WHAT THEY DIDN'T TEACH YOU IN SEMINARY

25 LESSONS FOR SUCCESSFUL MINISTRY IN YOUR CHURCH

JAMES EMERY WHITE

BakerBooks
a division of Baker Publishing Group
Grand Rapids, Michigan

Published by Baker Books
a division of Baker Publishing Group
P.O. Box 6287, Grand Rapids, MI 49516-6287
www.bakerbooks.com

Printed in the United States of America

Library of Congress Cataloging-in-Publication Data
White, James Emery, 1961–
    What they didn't teach you in seminary : 25 lessons for successful ministry in your church / James Emery White.
        p.   cm.
    Includes bibliographical references (p.   ).
    ISBN 978-0-8010-1388-1 (pbk.)
    1. Pastoral theology. 2. Church management. I. Title.
BV4011.3.W447 2011
253′.2—dc22   2011003213

11   12   13   14   15   16   17   7   6   5   4   3   2   1

In keeping with biblical principles of creation stewardship, Baker Publishing Group advocates the responsible use of our natural resources. As a member of the Green Press Initiative, our company uses recycled paper when possible. The text paper of this book is composed in part of post-consumer waste.

WHAT THEY
DIDN'T TEACH
YOU IN SEMINARY

Dedicated to the family of faith
known as Mecklenburg Community Church

Contents

Foreword

Perry Noble

'm a seminary dropout.

Wait! I did not say I am anti-seminary; in fact, I think that some seminaries still offer some value to those who are seeking to enter vocational ministry.

It's just that for me, well, I had a different experience.

I was well on my way in regards to what I refer to as the traditional trajectory when it comes to ministry. I received Christ and soon after entered college, where I received a four-year degree. After that my plans were to attend seminary, earn my MDiv, and then enter the full-time ministry.

But things didn't quite turn out the way I planned them.

I did finish college; however, upon completion I was offered a full-time job in a Baptist church where I had served in a part-time capacity during my senior year of college, and I took it, adjusting my plans from attending seminary full time to attending part time, one day a week, with a group of other pastors.

To say I was excited about diving into a theological and practical education that would prepare me for greater things in ministry would be an understatement. I was about to go out of my mind and just knew that what I was about to experience would change me forever.

It did . . . but once again things didn't turn out quite the way I planned them.

Within a few weeks of starting my experience in Christian higher education, we began diving into deep theological concepts such as limited atonement, the trichotomy and dichotomy of the Spirit, and the peccability versus impeccability of Christ.

However, what I was learning in the classroom and what I was actually experiencing on the front lines of ministry were completely different.

No one in the church seemed to be obsessed with whether or not Jesus could have sinned; they just knew that their marriage was in deep trouble and wanted help.

No one in the church was fascinated with my TULIP acrostic and the way I could present both sides of the argument; they just wanted to understand why in the world God would let their loved one die.

The leaders in the church did not care if I knew brilliant theological terms and could lecture them on church history; they just wanted to make sure that I was going to set a realistic budget for my area of ministry and then stay within the framework of that budget for the entirety of the year ahead of me.

I said it earlier, but please allow me to restate it again: what I was learning in the classroom and what I was actually experiencing on the front lines of ministry were completely different.

So I dropped out. I could list several reasons why; however, the main one was that I personally did not want to continue to invest hundreds of hours of my time and thousands of dollars into something that in the end would not adequately equip me for what I knew I would be facing in the "real world" known as ministry.

That is why I am so excited about the book you are now holding in your hands. My friend and mentor Dr. James Emery White is someone who I would call an "expert" when it comes to the academic *and* the practical world; he has walked in both of them and sees the value in each.

Dr. White's realization that seminary, while it does provide some value, does not adequately equip men and women for the ministry has led to what you will read in the pages that follow.

Honestly, I believe that the information contained in this book is more practical and empowering than nearly anything I ever experienced in the seminary setting. The stuff that he writes about really does happen—and if people are not prepared for it, then it will either knock them for a loop or, worse than that, cause them to either drop out or disqualify themselves from the ministry.

This is not a book to be simply read through and then stuck on a shelf but rather one that should be studied and discussed among church leaders and the people they serve with. I thoroughly enjoyed reading it and can say that even as a twenty-year ministry veteran, I was greatly stretched and sharpened by its words.

Perry Noble
Senior Pastor, NewSpring Church
Anderson, South Carolina

Acknowledgments

I wish to thank the Baker team for their support of this project, specifically Robert Hosack.

I have been greatly blessed by the support of three women for this project: my longtime assistant, Glynn Goble; Alli Main, who has begun partnering with me on book projects in innumerable ways; and my lovely wife, Susan, who once again made every page possible.

I also wish to thank the two seminaries that have most influenced my life: The Southern Baptist Theological Seminary in Louisville, Kentucky, and Gordon-Conwell Theological Seminary, with campuses in Massachusetts, Florida, and North Carolina. You have bestowed degrees, professorships, and even a presidency on my life. The book on what I *did* learn in seminary—as a student, professor, and administrator—would be too long to write.

This book is dedicated to the family of faith known as Mecklenburg Community Church in Charlotte, North Carolina. Since I've been their founding and senior pastor for twenty of my nearly thirty years of vocational ministry, most of what I have learned has been at their expense.

Introduction

What They Never Taught Me in Seminary

What they never taught me in seminary—sounds like I'm going to pick a fight. I'm not.

My life has been lived largely in two vocational worlds: the church and the academy. I am the founding and senior pastor of a church; I am a professor and former president of a seminary. So I would only be picking a fight with myself.

More than that, I loved seminary. I loved learning about church history and theology, philosophy and ethics. My pulse quickened the first time I was able to stand behind a podium and say, "In the Greek, this word means . . ." I loved building my library with works from Augustine to Zwingli. Adding entire multivolume reference sets, such as Kittel's *Theological Dictionary of the New Testament*, made my hormones bubble.

I was the classic three-year, residential MDiv student. But toward the end of my seminary studies, just before I started my doctoral work, I received a call from a church near the school asking me to consider coming as their interim pastor. It was an established denominational church in a county seat town near the seminary. The interim turned into a full-fledged invitation to serve as their senior pastor.

Some of you grew up in the church, so you had some experience with the inner workings of church life. Not me; I was pretty much unchurched for most of my life until the age of twenty. Even after I gave my life to Christ, I didn't get involved in the life of a church until a year or so before heading off to seminary. Thus when I, as a new pastor, was asked to officiate my first wedding, my first funeral, my first baptism, and my first communion, I was totally clueless. So why did they ask me to be a pastor in the first place in order to do such things? It was assumed that since I was nearing my graduation from seminary, I knew what I was doing.

I didn't.

So in panic mode I ended up buying every "minister's manual" the local Christian bookstore offered.

It didn't get any better.

I needed to raise money to meet the church's budget, and I had never had a class on that. I wanted to try to grow the church numerically by reaching out to the unchurched, and my course work had never touched on it. I had a problem with a combative and disagreeable deacon, and I searched through my seminary notes and found nothing. I found I needed to be in the office for administration, in my study to prepare my talks, in people's lives to stay connected to the community, and in my home to raise my family—and there hadn't been any instruction on how to manage that.

It was becoming painfully clear how little my seminary education had actually prepared me for the day-in, day-out responsibilities of leading a church.

I knew about the Council of Nicea, but no one had ever told me how to lead my *own* council meeting. I knew about the Barth-Brunner debate but not how to handle the breakdown between two Sunday school teachers when one was asked to start a new class, for the same age group, from the existing class. I knew the significance of the aorist verb but not how to parse the culture to know how best to communicate. I could tell you the leading theologians of the sixteenth century but not about leading and managing a staff.

This is why so many people look back on their seminary education with a critical eye. It's why pastors will go to a two-day leadership conference headlined by seasoned pastors passing on their insights for effective ministry and feel like they gained more in those two days than they did in their entire three years of seminary education. It's why quickly after graduation, Melanchthon gets dropped for Maxwell, Luther for Lucado, and the seminary's continuing education program for the latest megachurch conference.

Like so many others, I had gone to seminary to prepare for ministry, and I was not prepared for ministry. I was prepared academically to begin a life of teaching, which is, of course, invaluable. But in terms of the vocation of ministry beyond teaching? And even in regard to teaching, how to teach *effectively*? Not so much. Even worse was how ignorant I was about the *life* of ministry. I did not know how to manage my time, care for myself spiritually, or raise my kids in a way that was sane.

In other words, I never learned to do the things that I would actually have to be doing every day for the rest of my life.

We need seminary. But in fairness to a seminary education, there are certain things it will never be able to impart, even if it tries. God bless professors, but most of them have never been the pastor of a church. They may have been interim pastors or had a short-term pastorate while in seminary, but they are, in truth, academics. They are not *practitioners*. We need them, and we need the academic education they give us. But we also need what they *don't* teach you in seminary. We need insights and wisdom on leadership and relationships, emotional survival and communication, hiring and firing, sexual fences and our struggle with envying the pastor across town. We need best principles about money and time, decision making and church growth.

And we need it from someone who has done it. We need the raw street smarts that can only come from someone who has been educated in the trenches.

This is why the United States Army has instituted a complete overhaul of its basic training regimen—the first such revision in three decades. Largely as a result of what has been learned from Iraq and Afghanistan combat veterans, the army is dropping five-mile runs and bayonet drills in favor of zig-zag sprints and exercises that hone core muscles. Why? Because soldiers need to be prepared for what really happens in war. And in today's world, the nature of conflict has changed, and it demands a new kind of fitness. Modern combatants must be able to dodge across alleys, walk patrol with heavy packs and body armor, or haul a buddy out of a burning vehicle. Soldiers need to become stronger, more powerful, and more speed driven. They have to know how to roll out of a tumbled Humvee. They have to know how to crawl for their weapons. Sergeant Michael Todd, a veteran of seven deployments to Iraq and Afghanistan, said, "They have to understand hand-to-hand combat, to use something other than their weapon, a piece of wood, a knife, anything they can pick up."[1]

So from someone who loves and appreciates what a seminary education offers but who's been deployed in the war for a while, here's what they never taught me while I was there—and in fairness, never could.

16

1

Emotional Survival

Qualifications of a pastor: the mind of a scholar, the heart of a child, and the hide of a rhinoceros.

Stuart Briscoe

I was having coffee with a fellow pastor who needed more than caffeine to pick himself up. Summer attendance was down. Key people were leaving because of disagreements about the direction of the church. And money was very, very tight.

I felt nothing but empathy. *Yep, been there, felt that.*

"Jim," he said, "I knew seasons like this would come. I just didn't know how stressful they would be."

Neither did I. To this day, the disappointments can still blindside me. Nothing prepares you for how ministry can drain you emotionally, leaving you in pain or, even worse, feeling numb or in despair or with seething anger. This is why so many good men and women in ministry have careened into moral ditches and many more still soldier on with plastic smiles and burned-out souls.

A few years ago, my wife Susan and I were part of a mentoring retreat with about a dozen couples, all well-known leaders of large and thriving churches. We started off with an open-ended question: "What are your key issues right now?"

As we went around the room, the recurring answer in each of their lives was "emotional survival." We shared our stories about the hits and hurts that come our way in ministry as occupational hazards and how they tear away at our souls, sapping our enthusiasm, our creativity, and our missional stamina. They leave us dreaming of finding ourselves on a beach with a parasol in our drink—permanently.

What makes ministry so emotionally hazardous? That's easy. It all starts with overbuilt expectations. When you enter ministry, you can't help but dream. Many of us dream big. That's one of the marks of a leader—a compelling vision for the future. But for almost everyone, it's not long before the dream collides with reality.

When I planted Mecklenburg Community Church in the fall of 1992, I just knew (though I wouldn't have said so) that we would be a church in the hundreds, if not approaching a thousand, in a matter of weeks. Willow Creek, eat our dust.

The reality was starting in a rainstorm with 112 people, and by the third Sunday, through the strength of my preaching, looking out at 56 folks. Actually, 15 or 20 of those were kids in another room, so maybe 40 were actually in worship. Yes, our numbers did eventually increase, but I don't care what kind of growth you have—you usually had hoped for more.

Then there are the day-in, day-out realities of serving in a church that is very real, very flawed, and very challenging. No matter how well it goes, you have problems, issues, hassles, struggles, defections, setbacks, barriers, and defeats. You have to live with a level of quality about ten miles below what ignited your dream. Coupled with this is the work—hard work—and you realize that it could take years for even a glimpse of your dream to become reality.

And those are just the emotional hits from your expectations. Then there are the hits that come from the people you are working so hard to serve. This is the heart of the emotional drain. We are shepherds, and sheep are messy. Unruly. Cantankerous. Smelly. They are a chore to care for. And they can hurt you more than you could imagine—in particular, through the relational defections of those you trusted and the crushing crises from those who throw you into disaster mode.

You'll understand if I change a few details in what follows. In fact, most of the stories I'll tell throughout this book will be altered a bit to protect the guilty.

It was a Friday night in July. We were getting ready to leave for a vacation the next morning, and the phone rang. It was one of our staff. For him to call me at home on a Friday, much less the night before I was leaving for a vacation, was not a good sign.

"Jim," he said, "I have a roomful of people here at my house. There's a crisis. They thought you had already left, so they came to me."

"What is it?" was all I could manage to say.

He gave me the name of another staff member and said, "Jim, they're here because they've discovered she's been having an affair." And then he named the man she was involved with, who happened to be on our worship team. Let's just call them Jane and Bob.

I collapsed on the side of the bed as I held the phone in my hands. Thus began one of the worst experiences of my life and of the life of our church. After a night of no sleep, the next morning I met first with Jane. Then I met with Bob.

So much for vacation.

It turned out to all be true, and it had been going on for several weeks. Jane ended up resigning, and Bob and his wife left the church. It rocked our church's world. And mine. The ripple effects were incredible.

On a purely organizational level, it tore the guts out of our then fledgling music ministry. She was the leader of our band, our main musician, and our lead female vocalist. Her husband was our tech person. Bob was our lead male vocalist, and his wife was our only keyboardist. Our band no longer existed. Suddenly we found ourselves using recorded tracks for our weekend services.

But that was nothing compared to the emotional hit. There was the pain of the two families with a husband and a wife who felt utterly betrayed. Then there was the pain I felt as a pastor. When something like this happens, you feel violated, sick to your soul. You feel sick as a leader to see this church that you'd lay down your life for suddenly ripped apart. And you are supposed to sew things back together.

But the greater emotional hit is how you can quickly become the enemy, the bad guy, the adversary. In these situations and so many others like it, no matter how you handle the folks involved, some people will think you went too far on the side of grace, and others will think you went too far on the side of discipline. Change the story, change the people, and it's often the same. Pastors get caught in the crossfire of people's messes and often become the scapegoat. It's like the first person to rush to the side of a dog that has been hit by a car. In the midst of the dog's pain and frenzy, the person can often count on being bit—even though they are only trying to help.

We got through it as best we could, and with as much truth and grace toward both parties as possible, but Bob and his wife left very upset with us. They felt Bob should have been allowed to return to the platform after just a couple of months of counseling, and they accused us of showing partiality to Jane because she was on staff. So in the end, after we had poured ourselves into them for their reinstatement and loved them as best we knew how, they rejected us and left angry, taking with them four or five families who were their close friends.

I felt like I had been kicked by a horse.

There are so many other emotional hits in ministry: the stress of finances (both personal and in the church); the unexpected departure of staff; the pain of letters that criticize your ministry; the pressure of people who want to redefine the vision, mission, or orientation of the church; the relentless torrent of expectations; and the agony of making mistakes. And then there's this little thing called your marriage and family.

So how do you manage your emotional survival?

First, the bad news: there's not a quick fix. Ministry is just flat-out tough and often emotionally draining. You won't ever escape the hits and the hurts. They come with the territory.

Now, the good news: you can develop a way of life that protects, strengthens, and replenishes you emotionally. You can cultivate a set of activities and choices that allow God to restore your soul. Some things are obvious, like regular days off and annual study breaks if you can get them. And you'll need to get a lot more savvy about people and how to deal with them, which we'll talk about later.

But for now, here are two choices I wish I had made much earlier in my life. They may seem far removed from what caused the emotional hit in the first place, but they are key to ensuring you have a full emotional tank and can keep putting gas into it for the long haul.

Clear Boundaries Regarding Giftedness

First, *how* you serve is critical. Ministry is tough enough. But if you consistently serve outside of your primary areas of giftedness, you won't last very long under the stress and strain that comes with the territory. I really don't hear this talked about very much, if at all. But there's something about large amounts of time spent serving against the grain of your natural gifting that saps your emotional and spiritual energy.

I do not rank very high with the spiritual gift of mercy, not to mention how that plays itself out in, say, extended pastoral counseling. If I had to invest in that area with ongoing, regular blocks of time, it would wipe me out. I've had to learn to be very up front with folks about my areas of giftedness and how those gifts are supposed to operate in the mix with other people's gifts in the body. That's because what happens in a church, even one where spiritual gifts are taught and celebrated, is that the pastor is still expected to have them all—and to operate in them all. The danger is that you'll let yourself try, and soon you'll be wiped out with little or no reserves for the daily toil.

Related to this is operating outside of your personality type. A surprising number of pastors are, ironically, introverts. It's not that they don't love people or aren't good with people—most are even charismatic in terms of their leadership and speaking ability—but they are, in fact, introverts in terms of emotional makeup. As a result, many pastors get their emotional energy from being alone. If such realities are not acknowledged and managed, you will find yourself emotionally spent and soon burned out.

Yes, even as a pastor, you need to guard how you serve.

Emotionally Replenishing Experiences

Second, I've had to learn to intentionally pursue emotionally replenishing experiences. When you hurt, if you don't find something God-honoring to fill your tank with, you'll find something that isn't God-honoring. Or at the very least, you'll be vulnerable to something that isn't. I am convinced this is why so many pastors struggle with pornography—it offers a quick emotional hit.

To prevent that, I've had to learn to do things that channel deep emotional joy into my life. For some folks it's boating, or golf, or gardening. For me it's travel, reading, time alone with family, and enjoying anything outdoors—particularly the mountains.

Several years ago, a man I had invited into my life in a mentoring relationship asked, "Jim, what do you do that really puts gas back into your tank? If you could do one thing that would rejuvenate you spiritually and emotionally, what would it be?"

I didn't have to think very long or hard. I knew the answer: "I would go to the mountains and be alone." For as long as I can remember, the mountains have held significance for my spirit and emotions that I cannot explain. Being there alone is particularly rich, as I gain my deepest emotional energies apart from others.

He said, "Good. You should do that once a month."

I laughed. "You've got to be kidding. Once a month? The mountains? I don't have the time! My life is too busy, too full, to put something like that into my schedule."

Then he said something I will never forget. "If you don't, you will end up in a ditch. You will burn out, lose your ministry, perhaps even your family, and become a casualty of the cause."

I knew he was right. I was already seeing the edges of my life fraying and knew how easily my world could unravel.

I went to the mountains.

My first trip found me staying in a budget hotel, just overnight, in the heart of the Blue Ridge Mountains. I remember it to this day. It was like water on a dry desert. I felt energy and emotional renewal flowing into the deepest recesses of my inner being. I came home walking on air. I entered our foyer, hugged my kids, and kissed my wife. She thought I had been drinking. I had—from the well of emotional renewal from which God intends for all of us to take deep draughts of living water.

Now I escape to the mountains to a little bed-and-breakfast monthly. Every month I leave on a Thursday afternoon, and as I drive toward the cool air and clear skies, I feel the weight of the world fall off my shoulders. I feast off of it for weeks. Four, to be exact, until I venture to my precious emotional retreat once again.

On the front end I would have told you that it was impossible to put this into my life. Looking back, I will tell you that it is unthinkable not to have it.

So here's my question for you: If you could do one thing that would rejuvenate you emotionally, what would it be?

Now here's my challenge: for your sake, and your ministry's, do it.

2

The Five *C*'s

Jesus went up on a mountainside and called to him those he wanted.

Mark 3:13

I am often invited to facilitate leadership gatherings that are designed as large-scale mentoring sessions. I love the give-and-take, the back-and-forth, the questions and (hopefully helpful) answers.

Time and again I have found, through both personal experience and formal surveys of participants, the biggest issue facing those in ministry has to do with staff and volunteers. In other words, the people you have to work with.

The famed business author Jim Collins has written about getting the right people on the bus and then in the right seats.[1] When you don't, the organization suffers. So does the leader.

So how do you hire the right people and solicit the right volunteers? I have learned to follow five "*C*'s"—five things to look for in any hire or any volunteer. Violate them at great peril. I know—I've screwed up every one of them at one time or another, and I paid dearly. That's how I learned them.

Character

The foundational thing to look for is character. I know, we're all sinners, but I'm not talking about perfection. I'm talking about whether the person has a foundational ethic that operates in his or her life. It's often said that integrity is who you are when no one is looking. I want people I don't have to look after.

I am often asked about which character issues to overlook and which to make nonnegotiable. A serial predator who has a trail of dalliances in his background has, for me, a disqualifying character flaw. A person who never pays her bills on time due to habitual misuse of funds has a disqualifying character flaw. A person who manifests an ongoing pattern of deceit has a disqualifying character flaw.

The key words here are *habitual*, *pattern*, and *ongoing*. And I am particularly oriented toward the sins of the spirit, not the flesh. Yes, gluttony matters, but not as much for ministry as pride; yes, slipping up and having one too many glasses of wine is not optimal for those who feel the freedom to imbibe, but it pales in comparison to anger, envy, or sloth.

The reason character matters so much is because you cannot teach it. You cannot "impute" it (a good old King James English word) into someone. It's either there or it isn't.

Competence

The second dynamic to look for is competence. This has to do with the raw capability, the essential skills, needed to do

26

a job. This is the least of the five, as it is the one thing that can indeed be taught.

I have hired countless people who had no background in ministry. In many ways, I like this. They bring their personal, educational, and corporate skills to the table without preconceived notions regarding the practice of ministry. The basic competencies needed vary from role to role, but generally I look for the ability to get along with others, enthusiasm, a positive attitude, and raw leadership gifts.

Catalytic

A third area is one I seldom hear talked about but one that is increasingly important to my thinking—namely, that the person be catalytic. What I mean is that they create activity, bring energy, and have a spring in their step that makes things happen. I often use the word *hungry* or *aggressive* to characterize them. This can be misunderstood. I do not mean they are overly ambitious as much as they are driven by a deep desire to have their one and only life count.

When I describe such people and how I look for them for my teams, many leaders turn a horrified face toward mine. "How do you control them? How do you make sure they don't do something you don't want?"

My reply is always the same: I would rather rein someone in than have to continually kick-start them into gear.

Chemistry

A fourth issue has to do with chemistry, which is simply asking yourself, "Do you like them?" Yes, that's a legal question.

At our church, Meck, we have a little thing called the "beer test." Sorry if that offends you, but it's just a way of cutting to the chase about where you stand with someone and has little to do with whether you feel free to drink a Heineken or not. Here's how it goes: At the end of a long, hard, grueling day of work together, would you like to go out and have a beer with this person? If the answer is yes, they pass. If the answer is, "Are you kidding? The last thing in the world I would want is to see their face," they fail.

Think about how you feel when someone puts their head in the door on a Tuesday morning—are you glad to see them? Or does their very persona suck the life out of you? When you check your email and you see something from them, do you get a good feeling or bad? Do you read it first or dread even opening it?

I make no apologies for hiring people I like. Life is too short to put yourself into a team that doesn't work. I want to walk into each day enjoying the people I have to work with most intimately. More importantly, good chemistry results in good teams and effective ministry.

Called

Finally, they should be called to ministry. I know, you assume this, but don't. Many people are drawn to work in a church because they think it will be easy or serve a season of life when they need flexibility with kids, or because they are simply out of work and it seems readily available.

The goal is calling: that they would do it whether they were paid or not.

I recall a time when we needed to transition three part-time roles in a certain ministry to one or two full-time roles. The growth of the church and the demands of the ministry made it necessary. We just couldn't go part-time anymore. Further, two of those part-time people were somewhat questionable, it seemed, in regard to their commitment.

We communicated the decision, gave several months' advance notice, and cared for them well in terms of financial matters. We invited them to candidate for the full-time positions, though we suspected that their life stage would prevent them from pursuing the new roles.

Intriguingly, the two who seemed a bit passion challenged almost immediately left the church. It was not in anger; they just no longer felt it was the place for their church home. Translation: only the job was keeping them there. That's not a calling.

So here's the test for both sides: if you are only a member of a church because you work there, quit. You're not called. You may be called to ministry, even in the area you are currently serving, but if you would not attend that church independent of your employment, it's not a full calling. And if you know of someone on your staff who would not attend if they were not employed, and you are their supervisor, begin the exit strategy. Calling matters too much.

Farm League

So how can you make sure you have the five "C's" present and accounted for? Hire from the farm league.

I constantly counsel church leaders to hire from within. Most don't. Most look to other churches. They solicit résumés, work their networks, place ads. They go "potluck" and hope the person who passes the beauty contest is as good as they seem. They rarely are.

So what's the option? Look to your own church. Hire from within. View your current volunteers, the members who now serve in strategic roles, as your farm league.

Why is this best? *Because you know what you're getting.*
You know their character.
You know their competencies.
You know whether they are catalytic.
You know whether you have chemistry with them.
You know whether they have been called, at the very least, to your church.
Don't underestimate this.

But there's more. You know whether or not they "get it." Each church has a unique DNA, a focused mission, and a unique context. When you hire from within, you do not run the risk of contaminating the purity, force, and intent of your team. If you hire someone who continually walks around talking about how they did it at their old church, how much better things were at their old church, or how much better the leadership, teaching, and staff was at their old church, you'll be ready to send them back to their old church!

Yes, churches need "fresh blood" and new perspectives. You can gain quite a bit from someone's experiences in other venues. But you run an incredibly high risk of losing what you have worked so hard to create, namely, your church's unique DNA. So when we hire from the outside, we look to "sister" churches—places that share our philosophy of ministry, leadership style and structure, mission, vision, and values.

But before you make that outside selection, be sure to pick up the phone. More on that later.

3

The Next Next Thing

What has been will be again,
   what has been done will be done again;
   there is nothing new under the sun.

                              Ecclesiastes 1:9

The iPhone is so last month. Which means, observed the *New York Times*, that "it's been downgraded from the next big thing to merely new." And these days, "new can seem so yesterday. What matters is what's next." The article then noted how "next" is the go-to buzzword of our day.[1]

Newsweek's annual "Who's Next" issue, intended to run against *Time*'s "Person of the Year" issue, prompted *Time* to start a regular "What's Next" feature of its own. *New York* magazine had a cover article on home design titled "The Next Next Things," an update on the title of Michael Lewis's 1999 book *The New New Thing*. There are even stores specializing in the "next" through "fast fashion," such as H&M and Zara, which replace their entire line of clothing every few weeks.

Our preoccupation with "next" has replaced our earlier fascination with "new." The difference? "New" is what something is; "next" suggests a special insight.

Christians can be captivated by "next" as much as anyone. I know of pastors who joke about a "migratory flow pattern" among Christians in their community who are constantly church-hopping to the next thing in church life. They move from one church to another, looking for the next hot singles group, the next hot church plant, the next hot speaker, the next hot youth group. Many times they end up full circle where they began, because their original church suddenly became "next."

Church leaders can succumb to the same temptation, only in terms of church model. First it was Willow Creek. Then Saddleback. Then came Hillsong, Northpoint, and Fellowship. Or perhaps instead of doing it by church name, it was by type: first came seeker-targeted, then purpose-driven, then postmodern, then ancient-future, then emergent, then simple. For some the allure of the next "next" is programmatic, moving from Alpha to KidStuff to . . . well, you get the picture.

And then there is the latest "youth culture" report that boldly proclaims how radically different the next generation is going to be and how massive the changes will need to be if churches will stand a chance at reaching them.

But is the next really "next"?

Consider the widely disseminated window into the faith of young adults, or "Millennials"—so called because they are the first generation to come of age during the new millennium. According to the Pew Research Center, the headline is that these teens and twentysomethings are "less religiously affiliated" than previous generations. To be specific, one in four Americans age eighteen to twenty-nine do not affiliate with any particular religious group.[2]

However, as Stephen Prothero rightly observed in an essay in *USA Today*, this is not news. It is a "sociological truism that young people cultivate some distance from the religious institutions of their parents, only to return to those institutions as they marry, raise children and slouch toward retirement."[3]

Similarly, many of the "next" churches we flock to, as attenders or leaders, have little of the true "next" about them. More often than not, what is behind the attention is little more than a gifted communicator, or a niche focus, or tried-and-true contemporary approaches in a traditional context, or maybe one or two twists on previously envisioned programs—coupled with a growing edge of town. Yet the seduction of the "next" lures us to race to their conference to find the "secret" to success.

But racing toward the "next" is more than just deceptive—it can be dangerous. According to James Katz, who directs the Center for Mobile Communications Studies at Rutgers University, our current level of engineering knowledge allows products such as the iPhone to be developed more quickly than ever before. With basic performance less and less of a concern, consumers will purchase on the basis of looks. Add in what he calls "the professionalization of hype," and you have the life of a product burning hot—and fast.[4] That means you can buy into the next thing before you know whether it's even worth buying into. With an iPhone, you're only out a few hundred dollars. With a church, the stakes are much, much higher.

And even if this is not dangerous, it can be discouraging, particularly when the church you got the "next" from changes to the "next next" thing, and you are left high and dry trying to figure out what to do with the old "next."

Here's the critical question for the "next": Do you know *why* you are doing it? This is a pressing question for every church leader as they grapple with mission, strategy, and method in light of reaching out to an increasingly post-Christian culture. There is a myth that churches are successful because they do certain things; in truth, churches are successful because they know *why* they do certain things. In other words, they have a clear missional target on the wall.

This is why the most effective churches lead the way for innovation, and those who borrow their innovations get frustrated when the church they copied drops what they copied for something even more innovative.

In *How the Mighty Fall*, bestselling business author Jim Collins poses a simple but profound question: If you were in organizational decline, what would be the signs? What made the question more pressing was Collins's early sense, later confirmed through his research, that decline is analogous to a disease, perhaps like a cancer, that can grow on the inside while you still look strong and healthy on the outside. He calls it "the silent creep of impending doom."[5]

One of the earliest signs is companies saying, "We're successful because we do these specific things." The more penetrating understanding and insight is this: "We're successful because we *understand why* we do these specific things and under what conditions they would no longer work."

This is the foundation for any and all innovation; otherwise you are simply gathering an assortment of tactics independent of a mission. Biblical fidelity is, hopefully, a given, but once you are confident you are working within those parameters, you must then determine why it is you do anything: What is the foundational nature of your mission? What are you trying to accomplish? Who are you trying to reach?

If you know why you are doing something, you know whether it is effective, and you are quick to discard things that no longer work. If you are attempting to evangelize the unchurched, you are not attracted to any and all innovation, or even to innovation that may reflect the culture of the unchurched. Instead, you are after innovation that is effective at *evangelizing* the unchurched.

There have been and will be some truly "next" churches. But our threshold should be more than rapid growth, a charismatic leader, a niche market, or being the latest beneficiary of a growing edge of town or the migratory flow of believers. This is not simply because there may not be anything truly "next" about it beyond that which is cosmetic, but because our appetite for the "next" has us looking to churches that have yet to truly prove themselves, much less their ideas, through the test of time.

Leaders must realize that however exhilarating a new church model may appear, silver bullets do not exist. Leaders must look deeper than the latest model or program, conference or style, and realize that the process inherent within a thriving church has not changed in two thousand years: you must evangelize the lost, then assimilate those evangelized, then disciple those assimilated, and then unleash those discipled for ministry.

Ministry from Imagination

I'm not sure whether this idea is original to me or if I heard it somewhere else and the source has been displaced in my memory. But knocking around in my mind for some years has been the idea that we can do ministry from one of three standpoints.

For some, it's done through memory. They do it the way they have seen it done before, were trained to do it, or have seen it done in other settings. They do what they know to do and little more.

Others do it through mimicry. They gravitate toward a model of ministry that is attractive to them or exudes levels of success they long to experience. They absorb that approach and mimic it.

The dilemma with doing ministry from memory or mimicry is that it is not "alive." If you operate solely from memory—the way you've always done it before—then you are caught in the past. If you operate by mimicry, then you are caught in someone else's snapshot. They are doing ministry in a particular way, at a particular time, and in a particular context. There is value, to be sure, in learning all you can from their snapshot, but in time it may not be of ongoing value. Or it may not translate well to your context.

Solution? Do ministry not from memory or mimicry but from imagination. This means you are the originator, the creator, the one who is fashioning new solutions and opening new vistas. Born through earnest prayer and hard work, imagination is what keeps you from trying to chase the next next thing—and makes you instead become the one offering it.

4

Money, Money, Money

A wise man should have money in his head, but not in his heart.

Jonathan Swift

I once read about a man who phoned a church and asked if he could speak with the "Head Hog at the Trough."

The secretary said, "Who?"

"I want to speak to the Head Hog at the Trough!"

"Sir," she replied, "if you mean our pastor, you will have to refer to him with more respect."

"Oh, I see," the man said. "Well, all I wanted to do was talk to him about this ten thousand dollars I want to give to the church."

"Hold on," the secretary said. "I think the Big Pig just walked in the door!"

There's an old line that asks, "How much ministry can you do for a dollar?" Answer: one dollar's worth. Churches are totally dependent upon the generous contributions of those who follow Christ. This shouldn't be a problem, as the Bible clearly teaches Christ-followers to be generous and to start their generosity with a tithe of all that they earn to the local church of which they are a part.

But it doesn't always turn out that way. And even if it did, you would still have to *work* with money.

Pastors find that they have to develop budgets, lead capital campaigns for expansion, institute long-range financial planning, navigate salaries and benefits . . .

And you thought all you had to do was preach.

Making things worse is that one of the most gaping holes in almost everyone's seminary education has to do with money. It just doesn't quite fit the curriculum of church history, theology, biblical studies, and homiletics. A theology of stewardship? Maybe. Spreadsheets? Not likely.

But a financial education is one every church leader needs, and needs from day one. So here are five foundational money lessons I've gathered over the years.

Teach on It

First, you must, must, *must* teach on money. Most people think that one of the cardinal rules in church life is to be sure to *not* talk about money. The conventional wisdom is that it turns people off, and you want to turn people *on*. That's a dangerous half-truth, and it has killed church after church that desperately needed someone to stand up and talk about money.

Here's the truth about people and money. People are incredibly interested in issues related to their personal finances. That's why they subscribe to magazines about it, go to seminars on it, buy books about it, visit websites devoted to it, and log on to their financial accounts daily. They want to know how to manage their finances in a way that serves them and, as they grow in their spiritual lives, honors God. In fact, many of them are in deep financial trouble and would count financial life change among their deepest of felt needs.

The reason people hate it when the church talks about money is because of the *way* the church has talked about money. We have had a one-word vocabulary: *give*. We've had one way of talking about that word: guilt. We've had one concern when we turn on the guilt for the ask: self-serving institutional needs. So the problem isn't money; it's just how we've been dealing with it.

When someone attends and is instantly pressured to give, put on a guilt trip if they don't, bombarded with great big red "giving" thermometers on the wall related to the latest capital campaign, and told they can look forward to the annual ten-week series "Tithe or Burn," it turns them off.

This is one of the reasons why so many contemporary churches have started to tell guests not to feel obligated to participate in the offering. They say, "Let this service be our gift to you. We are much more interested in you than what's in your wallet." The negative ethos was so strong it needed to be defused.

So how *do* you bring it up? First, help them to see that giving is a matter of the heart. Show that it's more about *them* than it is about the church and its needs. They need to give to honor and worship God. We must convey the deeply biblical idea that where your treasure is, there your heart is also. That's probably the most important move you can make and your most important money message. It's the heart of discipling someone in regard to stewardship.

Second, make the teaching *comprehensive*. This means that your teaching about money isn't simply about tithing but is also about savings, debt, retirement, wise choices, materialism, greed, and envy. Help people with their finances by showing them how real and relevant the Bible is to the day-in, day-out issues they face with their money. Most of them are so strapped and so leveraged that they can't even see daylight. The Bible is rich in financial guidance and counsel and insight—share it with them, help them apply it to their lives, and let them see how God can impact their financial world when they place it under his leadership.

Finally, when you talk specifically about giving, make sure that you teach them how much it matters—to them and to others. It is a *very* dynamic act. For example, let them see how giving will make an enormous impact on their personal lives. The Bible teaches some clear things about God's blessing on their lives if they are generous and tithe, and giving will also provide adrenaline to the growth of their hearts for the things of God. Don't let the excesses of the "health and wealth" gospel keep you from teaching the real, true blessings that *can* come.

They should also be taught how much giving matters to the kingdom. Electricity bills don't get people too excited, but if that's all people see in terms of their giving and the church, they haven't been taught well. They need to be told what that electricity bill *does*. They're not really giving to the electricity bill; they're giving to the comprehensive needs of the revolution that God is leading, and through their gift, they're playing a part in that revolution. What I'm really talking about is vision casting, which is simply helping people get excited about what's going on so they want to be a part of supporting it.

The first large sum of money I ever had to raise was for the eighty acres of land on which our church now sits. When we raised the money for our land, one of the things I said loud and clear—and I meant it—was that I couldn't care less about the land itself. I had no need for a big campus, or big buildings, or anything like that.

I told people that when I thought about the land, I thought about the lives that would be changed, the marriages that would be saved, the children who would be taught about Jesus.

I meant it.

Encourage First Steps

A second lesson that is absolutely essential is to be sure to encourage first steps that people take toward financial faith and obedience. Whenever a person makes that first, small step toward God's leadership over their money, they should get a round of applause. Just like a toddler who takes his first step, when someone gives for the first time, they should get praised!

For example, send a special thank-you note to tell them how much their gift matters. And then, because their step is so important for their life and you're so encouraged by what they've done, send them a free set of recordings of a sermon series on overall financial management that you may have given in the past or a book that celebrates the life of the giver.

Now, that sounds like a lot to do for a first-time donor, but making that first gift is a big step for folks, and they need to be encouraged and thanked. What you are trying to do is take that small flicker that prompted them to give and fan it into a flame of stewardship. By the time you add up the cost of the paper, postage, CDs, and time it takes to send them, many times it's more than their gift. But it's an investment in them, and one that is worth it—not just in terms of the support it will bring to the church and its ministries but in terms of the growth of their spiritual life.

Related to this is how you teach about moving toward the biblical tithe. I believe in helping people start where they are and then move toward a full tithe. As mentioned, many people come to Christ with their financial lives in a wreck. Giving 2 or 3 percent would be nothing less than sacrificial. Helping them be responsible to their creditors (which is also biblical) as well as generous is often a process. So we help people get out of debt and *build* toward a tithe.

I'll never forget a thirtysomething man who stopped me after a service to say, "I'm there!" I didn't know what he was talking about at first until he added, "I'm finally at a tithe!" It had taken him over two years, but he had reached the point of being debt-free and generously giving.

Integrity

A third lesson, one that is absolutely essential for any church, is to handle money with integrity. There can't be even a hint of anything that might be out of sorts.

So first, if you haven't already, get a bookkeeper, fast. Let him or her handle the money, not you.

Second, move toward a congregationally approved operating budget as quickly as possible. If that's not your church polity, then get whatever governing authority you have to approve it. Somebody needs to be looking at your budget besides you and giving it a thumbs-up.

Third, get someone else to set your salary, even if you're a church planter. When Meck started, I pulled aside a group of men to set my starting salary and benefits so that even from day one I could say that I had nothing to do with what I made. Now my salary is set by trustees, members who are set aside and voted on by the church for that task.

A fourth way to build integrity (and this is the one that I think might matter the most) is to have an annual audit of your books from an outside accounting agency. Then let people know about that audit and make the results available to anyone interested. We have done that from day one, and it has bred confidence and a profound sense of integrity. The church at large has an awful reputation when it comes to money, and this allows you to be proactive in combating that image.

Be Positive

The fourth money lesson is to be positive when you talk about money and the needs you face. Nobody wants to give to a losing cause, so when you talk about money, talk about it in positive tones. People give to make a difference. They give because they're excited about what's going to happen with their gift. Doom and gloom doesn't motivate.

Let's say you're going to invest in a basketball team. Do you want to invest in one that is going downhill or one that is looking to make the playoffs this year? You want to invest in a winner, right? It's no different with a church. Don't lie, by any means, but do try to be positive.

I went to a church once where the pastor got up and said, "Folks, we've got a problem. Money, that's our problem. Money."

He was just warming up. "See these lights?" he asked as he gazed up at the ceiling. "Well, you won't be seeing them much longer, because we won't have the money to pay our light bill. Feel that air conditioning? Feels nice, doesn't it? Well, you won't be feeling that for much longer."

I kid you not. On and on this guy went, going through just about every aspect of the church's existence on life support. By the time he got finished, I didn't want to give. I wanted to pull the plug and put the church out of its misery.

The cup can be presented as half full or half empty, and people want to give to one that is half full.

Capital Campaigns Are Capital

Finally, you must resign yourself to the fact that you will have to lead your church through multiple capital campaigns throughout your ministry. It's the only way to buy land, build buildings, tackle huge kingdom endeavors, and make progress with the vision. Translation: it's how you turn vision into action. Without capital campaigns, you are consigned to incremental advancement—just running the ball up the middle, over and over, for a yard or two. With them, you can throw the ball down the field for massive yardage and run up the score.

We've used capital campaigns to buy an eighty-acre campus, build buildings to worship, serve children and youth, and disciple adults. We've been able to purchase land and build a house in the Philippines so that sex-trafficked children can be rescued from brothels. None of that could have been done through our general operating budget. We needed to challenge people to give *above* and *beyond*. In the Bible, this is called giving an offering. An offering was anything you gave above and beyond your tithe. A tithe was, in truth, considered to be the bare minimum anyone would even dream of returning to God, because that's what he had specifically asked for. So periodically, out of gratitude and commitment to God, people would give an offering above and beyond their 10 percent.

I used to dread the idea of a capital campaign. Now I relish giving people the privilege of making such a difference and seeing the kingdom ball advance so dramatically down the field.

Just call me the Big Pig.

5

It's the Weekend, Stupid

It's the economy, stupid!

James Carville

When Bill Clinton ran for the presidency in 1992, eventually scoring an upset victory over incumbent George H. W. Bush, his political strategist James Carville made it very clear what their overarching strategy would be. Hanging in every office was a singular sign for all to see: "It's the economy, stupid!"

And that really was the issue of the election. It would determine who won and who lost. Thanks to Carville, Clinton focused relentlessly on that issue. Bush didn't. Clinton won.

I once made a sign for our staff that you can still see hanging on cubicles and office walls around Meck. It too was simple. It read: "It's the weekend, stupid!" And it is.

The weekend is where guests experience you for the first time. It's where you have your largest gathering for impact.

So what matters most to the weekend? You might think it's the message. And yes, that matters, so much so that I'll give it its own chapter later on. But it's part of a larger picture. Remember, "It's the *weekend*, stupid," not "It's the message, stupid." The message is a part of the weekend, but only a part. I'm not talking theology here, or the centrality of the Word; I'm talking about the dynamics of throwing your doors open and inviting folks in. All the more reason to highlight the *other* four factors that will determine whether people actually hang around for the message.

Friendliness

The first is friendliness. In an interesting study, the Technical Assistance Research Program for the White House Office of Consumer Affairs found that 96 percent of unhappy customers never complain about rude or unfriendly treatment, but 90 percent of those unhappy persons will not return to the place where that unfriendliness was manifest. Furthermore, each one of those unhappy persons will tell nine other people about the lack of friendliness and courteousness, and 13 percent will tell more than twenty other people.[1]

A later study by the same organization discovered that the number one reason why individuals do not return to a particular establishment is an indifferent, unfriendly employee attitude.[2]

Now, every church thinks it's friendly. I've never met a church yet that said, "Yeah, we're mean as sin and proud of it!" No! Every church *thinks* it's friendly. But what that means is

- they are friendly to each other;
- they are friendly to people they know;

- they are friendly to people they like; or
- they are friendly to people who are like them.

That's not friendliness; that's a clique or, at best, a club.

People today are hungry for relationship, hoping for a network of people to be family and friends. You have to reach out, include, and accept for the sake of Christ. This needs to be cultivated to become part of your DNA. That's why you should start an entire ministry around it, if you haven't already. We call ours "Guest Services," and it oversees greeters, ushers, hospitality, and so much more—all geared toward the experience of friendliness and acceptance. At Meck, it's one of our largest and most strategic efforts. It actually envelops a two-mile radius around our campus; on a weekend, we want to reach out and welcome people in.

Children's Ministry

The second of the big four has to do with your children's ministry.

Several summers ago my family and I went to a church while on our study break. It was a new church, very small, that was meeting in a movie theatre. How can I say this? It was . . . one of the most programming-challenged services I've ever attended. It was so bad that we were looking at our watches *five minutes* after the service started. When the service mercifully ended, we wanted to get out of there and never return.

But when we went to pick up our then very young kids, they were having an absolute blast. They didn't want to leave! A young couple had just poured themselves into that ministry and made it really, really good. I still recall how they had transformed a meager space into a time machine, complete with special effects music, that took the kids back into Bible times. New kids, such as ours, were treated extra special and taken to a treasure chest full of small toys from which they could choose.

We went to some of the best churches in the area that summer, but our kids *pleaded* with us to take them back to the one we could barely stand. Now, if I lived there and felt compelled to find a church home as a father of four, do you think I would have at least given that church another try? You can count on it.

Here's the lesson: You can drop the ball in the service but ace it with the kids and have a chance that they'll return. But no matter how good the service is, if the children's ministry is bad, they won't come back—unless they're folks without kids.

Too many pastors treat children's ministry as a necessary evil. It's *severely* underfunded, understaffed, and underappreciated. Wake up. Children are the heart of your growth engine.

Music

I loved *Sister Act*. I know, it's dated, but what a fun flick. When the character played by Whoopi Goldberg, a "nun on the run" if there ever was one, puts contemporary music into the struggling parish's services, the crowds pour in. The priest, confronting the Mother Superior's concerns about such outlandish tunes, admonishes her by simply saying, "That music. That wonderful music. It *calls* to them."[3]

And music does. And always has.

Let's not get into the "worship wars" stuff. But let's *do* be savvy. There is no such thing as traditional music. All music was at one time newfangled, contemporary, cutting edge, and probably too loud.

The great hymns of Martin Luther are considered traditional to our generation, but they were anything *but* traditional to the people of Luther's day. Many of the great hymns written during the Protestant Reformation, such as "A Mighty Fortress Is Our God," were based on barroom tunes that were popular during that period. Luther simply changed the lyrics and then put the song into the life of the church. The result? People were able to meaningfully express themselves in worship.[4]

Charles Wesley also borrowed from the secular music of his day, and John Calvin hired secular songwriters to put his theology to music, leading the queen of England to call them "Geneva jigs."[5] Bach provides a similar pattern, using the popular cantata for weekly worship music. He was also known to seize tunes from "rather questionable sources and rework them for the church."[6] Even Handel's *Messiah* was condemned as "vulgar theatre" by the churchmen of his day for having too much repetition and not enough content.[7]

The point? Throughout history you'll find a connection between church growth and contemporary music. I'm sorry if that's too crass for you, but it's true. Don't ever downplay music—don't forget, an entire book of the Bible is almost nothing but lyrics! So here are two words that will serve you well: music matters.

Building

The first impression of a guest begins long before the service ever does; it begins the moment the guest drives into the parking lot. It is at that moment—when they first view the church and its grounds—that the initial impression is made. And as the familiar phrase goes, you don't get a second chance at a first impression. Physical surroundings convey strong messages: if the lighting is inadequate, the message is "unfriendly"; if the equipment and facilities are out of date, the message is "irrelevant"; if the upkeep is poor, the message is "They haven't got it together" or, even worse, "This God they serve must not deserve better."

Let's get really practical. What is the parking lot like? Are the stripes clearly painted or faded with age? Is there trash strewn around? Are bushes and hedges trimmed? Is the grass neatly mowed? Is the church sign on the front lawn by the street in good shape, with letters neatly arranged with an appealing message or interesting information? Growing churches take their physical appearance with utmost seriousness. They understand that the environment in which someone worships directly affects their worship experience.

But physical surroundings are far more than the external appearance of the facilities. They include the internal state of the facilities as well.

Several years ago my wife and I moved from Louisville, Kentucky, to Nashville, Tennessee, having left the pastorate for a denominational position. Our family experienced what was for us a rare and interesting phenomenon: church shopping. At the time, my wife and I had three young children. As you might guess, the room of greatest interest to us was the nursery.

I am almost ashamed to tell you what we found in many churches: sheets on cribs that hadn't been changed in weeks; paint peeling off of the walls; toys in ridiculous disrepair and condition; poor lighting and ventilation; insufficient supervision. One church nursery was so bad that we could not in good conscience leave our youngest child in order to participate in the worship service.

The church we eventually joined, however, was vastly different. The sheets were changed after every use; toys were in excellent condition and disinfected between sessions; a teacher-child ratio was provided that was more than adequate; the lighting and ventilation was excellent; the carpet was immaculately cleaned and vacuumed. We left our kids and said, "Here they are—we'll see you in six months!"

Just kidding. We picked them up in three.

The principle of cleanliness extends to all areas of the church, such as the restrooms, vestibule, classrooms, and of course the front of the sanctuary. I have been in numerous churches where the front part of the sanctuary, where the eyes of all in attendance are focused for an hour or more, was anything but presentable.

After a seminar I led on such issues, a pastor came to me and said that he didn't think that he had ever sat in one of the pews in his church and examined the appearance of the front of the sanctuary. He later wrote me and shared that when he did, he was horrified at what he saw: hymnbooks strewn haphazardly all over the top of the piano and organ, old Sunday school quarterlies beside the pulpit, corners of the carpet frayed and worn, chipped wood on the furniture, and several burned-out lightbulbs. He wrote, "To think that our visitors were staring at that mess for over an hour!"

It has been said that familiarity breeds inattention, and this is certainly true in terms of the physical appearance and cleanliness of our churches. If you discover a crack in the mirror of your bathroom, your immediate reaction is one of horror and a resolve to see to its speedy repair. After a few busy weeks, you notice it again and make a mental note to see that it receives attention. After six months, you simply don't see it anymore. But your guests *do*.

Ray Kroc, the founder of McDonald's, paid a surprise visit to a Winnipeg franchise. It is reported that he found a single dead fly. The franchisee lost his McDonald's franchise two weeks later.[8] Another tale of Kroc's commitment to cleanliness tells how Kroc, on his way back to the office from lunch, asked his driver to pass through several McDonald's parking lots. In one of those parking lots, Kroc spotted some papers caught up in the shrubs along the outer fence. Immediately Ray went to the nearest pay phone and called the office, got the name of the local manager, and then called the employee to offer his help in picking up the trash in the parking lot. Later, both Ray Kroc, the owner of the McDonald's chain, and the young manager of the store met in the parking lot and got down on their hands and knees to pick up the paper.[9]

If that commitment exists in the secular world for the sake of profit, how much more should the commitment of God's people be for the sake of the gospel?

6

Sexual Fences

Can a man scoop fire into his lap without his clothes being burned? Can a man walk on hot coals without his feet being scorched?

Proverbs 6:27–28

Few people have maintained the moral integrity necessary for a lasting and influential public ministry better than Billy Graham. Without a doubt, he finished well. For that, you can thank the Modesto Manifesto.

In November of 1948, as his public ministry began to take hold, Billy called his cohorts George Beverly Shea, Grady Wilson, and Cliff Barrows to his hotel room during an evangelistic campaign they were holding in Modesto, California. "God has brought us to this point," he said. "Maybe he is preparing us for something that we don't know. Let's try to recall all the things that have been a stumbling block and a hindrance to evangelists in years past, and let's come back together in an hour and talk about it and pray about it and ask God to guard us from them."

When they gathered back together in Billy's room later that afternoon, they had all made essentially the same list. From it they made pledges, which came to be known among them as the "Modesto Manifesto," to guard themselves, among other things, against the two things most damaging to the cause: the inappropriate use and allure of money and, perhaps even more damaging than money entanglements, sexual immorality. For the latter, the rules were simple: they avoided situations that would put them alone with a woman. On the road, they roomed in close proximity to each other as an added margin of social control. And always, they prayed for supernatural assistance in keeping themselves "clean."[1]

Translation: Billy Graham built sexual fences around his life. And we need them every bit as much as, if not more than, Billy. Here are three such fences to consider.

Thought Life

First, monitor and control your thought life. That's where sexual sin begins. Things like adultery, in all its forms, don't just happen—they *begin*. We're in bed with someone mentally and emotionally *long* before we are in bed with them physically.

Ready to get real?

One of the most damaging fantasy worlds we can allow ourselves to enter doesn't even involve someone we may work with or minister to. It's an image on a computer.

When it comes to pornography, the question facing many men is simple: Is it really wrong? Is it really that big of a deal? I mean, it's just an image on a screen. It's not someone

I know (so it's not lust, right?) or someone I'm having an actual affair with, so I'm still faithful to my wife. It's just sexual release, like masturbation, and we all know that masturbation is not condemned in the Bible. It's not even mentioned. And isn't sex a good thing—so what's wrong with watching it happen? I'm just admiring beauty. And besides, I'm single, so what do you expect me to do with all this pent-up sexual energy? It seems like a safe release until I *am* married.

I've heard all of this and more. So is it really that big of a deal? Yes, and here's why.

It is sexual sin. Jesus made it clear that when we give in to lust, it is akin to the act itself. It makes no difference whether you know the person or not; lust is not tied to relationship.

It is addictive. The ubiquitous nature of porn is new to our culture and to human sexuality, but it is becoming increasingly clear that it is highly addictive in nature. As a result, it not only can begin to dominate a life but also can demand ever-increasing levels of exposure and ever-increasing degrees of experience to continue to stimulate.

It is degrading to women. In pornography, women are treated as objects. They are not fulfilling God's dream for their life as his precious daughter, nor are they fulfilling his design for sexual expression and fulfillment. You are watching a woman who is being sinned against by being treated in a way that is contemptible to her heavenly Father (whether she sees it that way or not—and the fact that many may not only adds to the tragic nature of porn).

It leads to other sins. Studies are beginning to show that the effect of porn on men is more than temporary sexual stimulation: as they see women treated as objects, they begin to treat women that way. They become more sexually aggressive, leading to date rapes and the expectation of "hookups." All that to say, what we *view* can quickly become what we *do*.

It harms your relationship with your current or future spouse. It is absolutely bogus to say that watching porn enhances a sexual life. Instead, it cheapens it. Porn quickly becomes a substitute for sexual intimacy with your spouse. It is a dose of novocaine into your sexual system, not a dose of Viagra.

It desensitizes your soul. Let's stay with this idea of novocaine. Sin of any kind desensitizes your spiritual life. Continued exposure to a sin such as pornography deadens you and grieves the Holy Spirit in your life, forcing him to withdraw his utmost filling in a way that diminishes his power and presence in your life.

Your body is a conduit of the Holy Spirit, which is why sexual sins matter so much—they can diminish the Holy Spirit's filling of your life. As the apostle Paul noted, "There is a sense in which sexual sins are different from all others. In sexual sins we violate the sacredness of our own bodies, these bodies that were made for God-given and God-modeled love, for 'becoming one' with another. Or didn't you realize that your body is a sacred place, the place of the Holy Spirit?" (1 Cor. 6:18–19 Message).

It distorts sex. As C. S. Lewis says in *Mere Christianity*:

You can get a large audience together for a strip-tease act, that is, to watch a girl undress on the stage. Now suppose you came to a country where you could fill a theatre by simply bringing a covered plate on to the stage and then slowly lifting the cover so as to let every one see, just before the lights went out, that it contained a mutton chop or a bit of bacon, would you not think that in that country something had gone wrong with the appetite for food? And would not anyone who had grown up in a different world think there

56

was something equally queer about the state of the sex instinct among us?[2]

There's not much I can add to that.

Vulnerable Situations

A second fence to erect is to be sure to avoid vulnerable or compromising situations. Again, let me get real nuts and bolts here, because it's important:

- Watch how and when you are alone with someone of the opposite sex.
- Watch how you touch people—be careful with your hugs and lingering touches.
- Watch how you interact with people—don't visit someone of the opposite sex at home alone.
- Watch out for that long lunch alone together or staying late and working together on the project.

This is just common sense, isn't it?

I think some people in ministry go further with this than may be necessary. They won't close doors in public office space; they won't have lunch in public areas with someone; they won't get in a car with someone of the opposite sex. I'm not about to argue over how high the fence should be; the greater danger is not having any fences at all. The point is being aware of situations that you know put you in a compromising position.

And let's state the *really* obvious: erect particularly high fences when you know you are already attracted to someone, because the temptation will be to take the fence down. If there is someone you think about a lot or someone you catch yourself comparing your spouse to in an uncomplimentary way, or if you are finding excuses to be with them (or be alone with them), or if you catch yourself having sexual fantasies about them, be *extraordinarily* careful.

Think Long Term

Finally, use your God-given brain to think long term, which is where we started this discussion. Left to themselves, your sexual urges will press you to seek immediate gratification, as if there are no long-term repercussions. If you don't engage your brain, you will endanger your marriage, undermine your values, risk your health, and trade away long-term happiness for short-term satisfaction.

In short, you will lose the life you now have. Your family, your ministry, your reputation. Everything. That's a sex drive without a driver.

Have you ever heard of the idea known as 10-10-10? It's not particularly original with anyone, though some have written formally about it.[3] It stands for ten minutes, ten months, and ten years, and it speaks to using your brain to address your life in a simple but life-changing way: What are the consequences of my decision in ten minutes, in ten months, and in ten years?

That kind of thinking is what your sexual impulses need. Left to themselves, they will only engage the first ten minutes. But it's the ten months and the ten years that matter most.

It'll Never Happen to Me

One of my favorite shows on ESPN is *Mike and Mike in the Morning*, featuring Mike Greenberg and Mike Golic. It's a joint radio and television broadcast about sports. "Greenie," as he is affectionately known, was formerly a sports reporter, and Golic played college football for Notre Dame and in the NFL for Detroit.

One morning, as they discussed one more celebrity athlete's misconduct off the field—after a season of stories ranging from Michael Vick's dogfighting to Tiger Woods's infidelity—Greenie asked Golic what athletes say to each other in the locker room when such news breaks about a fellow player. Golic said, "They say the same thing every time. They say, 'It'll never happen to me.'"

But it can.

Including you.

Every person can be tempted. *Every* person can succumb to that temptation. It is in our character. In fact, if you think you can't be tempted in this area, you are the most vulnerable of all.

Why? Because you are not humble enough to put up your guard.

7

Rabies of the Heart

I don't hate anybody. 'Cause the Bible says it's a sin to hate. But there are some folks I hope dies of cancer of the tonsils.

a Louisiana pastor[1]

We're going to have to have an agreement in order to proceed with this chapter. The agreement is total candor and transparency. Up for it? Let's see.

Can you think of the name of a pastor you would secretly enjoy seeing fail in ministry? A person who, in your darkest, most deliciously evil moments, you would enjoy seeing exposed in tomorrow's paper for having an affair, extorting money, or causing their church to split apart?

If you're going to be honest, you can. We all can.

Some pastors have a lot of pastor friends. They are not typical. Most pastors are very isolated from their peers and often at odds with them. Why?

They are the competition. And they feed into our darkest, least-talked-about disease: *envy*.

The Bishop of Alexandria

Irish writer Oscar Wilde once told a fictional tale about how the devil was crossing the Libyan desert. He came upon a spot where a small number of demons were tormenting a holy hermit. The sainted man easily shook off their evil suggestions. The devil watched as his lieutenants failed to sway the hermit, then he stepped forward to give them a lesson.

"What you do is too crude," he said. "Permit me for one moment."

He then whispered to the holy man, "Your brother has just been made Bishop of Alexandria." Suddenly, a look of malignant envy clouded the once-serene face of the hermit. Then the devil turned to his imps and said, "That is the sort of thing which I should recommend."[2]

No wonder Herman Melville called envy "the rabies of the heart."

Envy has its genesis when we see something desirable that belongs to another person. It could be physical appearance, a job, money, talent, position, a spouse, even children. The other person possesses something that we want. Envy is a vice of proximity—the closer someone is to us in terms of vocation, temperament, gifts, or position, the more fertile is the soil in which envy grows. In the classic pattern, notes theologian Cornelius Plantinga, the prosperous envier resents the rich, the one who runs a mile in 3:58 resents the one who runs it in 3:54, the pretty resent the beautiful, and the hardworking B+ student resents the straight-A student, especially the happy-go-lucky one who never seems to study.[3]

When you give in to envy, you not only desire what another person has and resent them for having it; you want to destroy its presence in the other person's life. What an envier ultimately wants is not simply what another has; what an envier wants is for another *not to have it.*

Most of the time this is subtle. For example, Chuck Swindoll says we can take the "but" approach. We say,

> "He's an excellent salesman, but he isn't very sincere."
> "Yeah, she's smart, but she doesn't have any common sense."
> "She's a good surgeon, but she doesn't mind charging you for it."

The "but" approach is utilized when we reluctantly acknowledge a particular gift in someone but then let envy quickly enter to destroy the other person's gift.

Schadenfreude

The subtle nature of envy's destructive bent is not always verbal, much less even active. There is a silent version of envy's destructive tendencies. Consider the secret satisfaction we experience at the misfortune of others. The Germans have a word for it: *schadenfreude*, which means finding joy in the suffering of another.

Do you revel in the success of another church? Do you enjoy it when the local newspaper features a story on something positive that they did?

Or would you have preferred to read about a downfall—declining attendance, a staff defection, a failed effort at outreach, or a scandal?

Let's be honest. We'd like the dirt. Sometimes we'll even participate in spreading it, being quick to share rumor and innuendo, gossip and hearsay. Why? We pathetically think it tears them down and builds us up.

Can we call it what it is? *Sin.* That leader is your brother or sister in Christ. You really are in this together. They are not the competition, much less the enemy. Satan is. Why can't we get this one right? It's so terribly destructive.

This is why the Bible warns us of the sin of envy in such strong language: "If you harbor bitter envy and selfish ambition in your hearts, do not boast about it or deny the truth. Such 'wisdom' does not come down from heaven but is earthly, unspiritual, of the devil. For where you have envy and selfish ambition, there you find disorder and every evil practice" (James 3:14–16).

And church leaders are as prone to it as anyone. In fact, we may be among the worst. Brace yourself—I'm going to go for the jugular.

The Largest and Fastest-Growing

It's become as anticipated among some pastors and ministry leaders as the annual *U.S. News and World Report* ranking of schools is to college and university presidents, the *Forbes* 500 is to CEOs, and the AP poll is to college sports coaches and fans. It is *Outreach* magazine's annual listing of the 100 largest churches and the 100 fastest-growing churches.

One year a member of our staff stuck his head in my office, referenced the latest listing, and said, "Shouldn't we have been in it?" Having already glanced at the list with undeniable curiosity and making a few quick mental calculations, I already knew the answer. "Yes, we would have been on the fastest-growing list, and fairly high up . . . but I didn't submit any of our numbers."

I could see it written on his face. "What were you think-ing? You didn't submit our numbers?" He knew that we were currently in the fastest-growing season in the history of the church. We had gone from three services to six, with a sev-enth planned for the spring, and were laying the groundwork for a major building expansion on our eighty-acre campus.

I found myself stumbling for the way to respond, but then it came out: "It just didn't feel . . . clean." There. I had finally said it, though I had felt it for a long time. The listing seemed dirty, competitive, dark—yes, for me, even sinful.

Let me hasten to emphasize, "for *me*." The darkness is entirely mine—my own long battle with competition, my own hot and cold embrace of a kingdom mind-set, my constant temptation toward schadenfreude over the demise of others, all along with a good dose of ongoing pride. I had crowed about our own numbers too many times in the past in ways that did not honor God but only honored me, and I had felt palpable shame. Like a man who battles lust finally giving in and openly poring over pornography on the internet or entering into an affair, for me to submit our numbers would feel like caving in to one of the more important spiritual battles in my life.

I am not trying to indict *Outreach* magazine, much less those who participated. I have no doubt they are good, well-intentioned folk who are attempting to serve the kingdom through this compilation. This is confession, not admonition. To be sure, I have sensed the way the list (and others like it) has been used by those who, it would seem, share in my darkness. Too many are too quick to anoint the "next thing," gloat over those with past success who are now experiencing decline, race to find the silver bullet of success, or take pride in their own success as if God has finally arrived. But that only adds to my disgust as I see my own struggles manifest in others.

So each year, it has almost become a personal spiritual discipline. The form arrives, I start to fill it in, and then I ask myself, *Why?*

It won't advance the cause of our mission at Meck; it won't help us reach lost people. It may open a few more doors of opportunity in terms of speaking platforms, but God can see to that in other ways if he so desires. The only motivation I could find was self-serving: to be noticed and then acclaimed. And that felt dirty.

For a long time I have been haunted by a single verse in the Old Testament that came from God through the prophet Jeremiah: "Should you then seek great things for yourself? Seek them not" (Jer. 45:5). Great things for God, yes; great things for myself, no. And the line between the two can often become conveniently blurred.

I love the church. I love the kingdom of God. I want to see it expand. I love that churches around the world are growing. But to single them out in a way that draws attention to them simply for their numerical growth and nothing else does not seem entirely healthy to me, as it offers a distorted view of success.

Crowns in heaven will not be based on numerical attendance, growth, acres, or even decisions to follow Christ. For pastors and churches, it will be based on faithfulness to the vision of the church as cast by the New Testament. God may use me, or someone else, to bear much fruit. But in the end, I suspect that a bivocational pastor in a small town of five thousand with an average church attendance of fifty may be the greatest pastor on the planet, with the largest crown in heaven.

You may see Meck's numbers in future lists in *Outreach* magazine, or you may not. We may not submit them, and even if we do, we may not warrant inclusion. But if you do see them, it could mean that I have either given in to my dark side—or somehow risen above it. The only reason I could swallow would be to somehow help Meck do the ministry God has clearly called it to try to fulfill. But what you will know for certain is that it means very little. It will not tell you whether we are turning attenders into disciples; it will not tell you whether we are creating a new culture in our city that honors Christ; it will not tell you whether we are attracting sheep from other churches or truly reaching the radically unchurched. It will just tell you that we got even bigger than we already are, or grew at an even faster clip, and on our worst days have way too big of a head about it and are way too fixated on who is ahead of us on the list.

Bottom line: don't compare yourself to other Christians, others leaders, and other churches—except to learn from them as mentors.

Remember how Jesus handled this?

Turning his head, Peter noticed the disciple Jesus loved following right behind. When Peter noticed him, he asked Jesus, "Master, what's going to happen to him?"
Jesus said, "If I want him to live until I come again, what's that to you? You—follow me." That is how the rumor got out among the brothers that this disciple wouldn't die. But that is not what Jesus said. He simply said, "If I want him to live until I come again, what's that to you?" (John 21:20–23 Message)

God will almost certainly have others live longer and do more than you—or me. The real issue?
"You—follow me."

8

Zero Tolerance

Fool me once, shame on you; fool me twice, shame
on me.

seventeenth-century proverb

Get a group of pastors together, at least any who have been
pastors for very long, and ask them what has caused them
the most heartache, the most grief, the most pain, and the
most discouragement. They'll say, "People."

Push them further, and these "people" will fall into two
categories: the ones who are draining, and the ones who are
damaging. This chapter is about the ones who are damaging.
I have one big piece of advice. It might startle you. It may
even seem radical.

Do what the Bible says to do.

Why is that so radical? Because what the Bible says to do is
about as counterintuitive to the average pastor as you could

67

possibly imagine. It doesn't even feel *legal*. Strange way to feel about the Bible, I know. But it's true.

We'll teach what the Bible says about everything else—and apply it—but for some reason, the clear directives about dealing with problem people in our lives as spiritual leaders is either ignored or just so uncomfortable that we refuse to consider it for our lives.

And the Bible's advice? Zero tolerance.

Now, let's be clear. I'm not talking about people you are allergic to. I don't mean high-maintenance people, needy people, or even the ones with whom you have such bad chemistry that the minute you see their face you feel the life sucked out of you. These are the draining ones. We'll get to them later.

But there is a set of behaviors, an attitude, that should be met with a "zero tolerance" mentality from you as a leader. There is something so destructive to the church and its mission that it must be met with a swiftness and firmness that ensures it is never allowed to take root. There is one thing that we, as shepherds charged to watch over a specific flock, are told to whack over the head with our shepherd staffs the second it appears.

No, I'm not talking about elders. Not even deacons.

I'm talking about this: "Warn a quarrelsome person once or twice, but then be done with him. It's obvious that such a person is out of line, rebellious against God. By persisting in divisiveness he cuts himself off" (Titus 3:10–11 Message). The one attitude, the one spirit, that you must meet with zero tolerance is that which fosters division and dissension in the church.

Why? Because it is so damaging. So much so that it was the one thing Jesus prayed against in his great High Priestly prayer before his crucifixion (see John 17). Jesus prayed for unity and love among those who would share his name because, he said, it would be the ultimate apologetic for his message.

Little wonder there is a zero tolerance mentality in the Bible toward those who would rip the church apart through dissension, disgruntlement, and division; through spreading false doctrine and hyping petty doctrine; through power plays and malicious gossip; through slander and the undeserved undermining of established leadership.

If you do not follow the Bible and confront these things, you do so at your peril. One of my biggest leadership mistakes cost our church at least three years of growth and forward progress. You have no idea how just writing that line makes me sick to my stomach. Three years!

My leadership mistake was simple but profound: I allowed a staff infection to take root that manifested itself in a spirit of division and dissension, and then I failed to confront it in a timely manner. As a result, it took hold and spread like a cancer, infecting people and teams, families and leaders in ways that in many cases were irreparable.

It started by hiring someone in violation of the "Five C's" (see chapter 2) and from outside of the church to boot. That was a double whammy mistake. There was no chemistry between us, and I would soon find out that emotional and relational maturity were absent in this staff member as well. Nor was he called to the church or our ministry—he was simply in need of a job and we were knocking on the door.

Why did I violate so many hiring principles? A phone call. A Christian celebrity called me and said that this man was available, highly gifted, and a real catch. The backstory was that they were friends from a similar church, the man had been laid off from a job, and his well-known friend was graciously trying to find a place for him to land. I fell for it.

I recall one of the first times I interacted with him. It was on a golf course. I'm not sure I ever saw him smile. He seemed fundamentally unhappy, as if mad at the world that he had to go slumming for work. And in his mind, that's what it was. I sensed that he was so taken with his one and only church experience, in one of the more well-known megachurches on the planet, that he would forever be finding us wanting. But I blew past these warning signs and more and brought him on staff.

From the onset he began to spread dissension. We were about to open a new wing to a building, and a volunteer made some kind of comment in his hearing about not doing something because "Jim wouldn't like that." Rather than seeing that as something potentially positive—that the volunteer was enforcing a value that she knew I would uphold as well—he automatically read into it an autocratic and dictatorial style. And he told the volunteer as much.

Over the next several months, he single-handedly spread more negative thoughts and vibes than any other person in the history of our church. His style was simple: where there had been no disappointment or disgruntlement, he planted the seed.

"Did you really think that was a good talk? Maybe if you're in a classroom. It was more teaching than communicating to me. Now my old pastor—he was a *communicator*."

"How did you feel about that meeting? Didn't seem like we had much say-so, did it? Where I came from, staff input was valued."

"You think the sky is blue today? This isn't very blue at all to me. You want to see blue, you should see where I came from. Our pastor really made it blue."

Okay, he didn't say the last one, but it would have fit.

Before I knew it, I was the worst speaker, the worst leader, the least community-minded, the least accountable . . . you get the picture.

What a person like this does is create discontent and dissatisfaction where it did not exist before. Or they take the weakest embers of such potential feelings and fan them into a flame wildly out of proportion to the reality at hand. Sadly, he found ample kindling.

We had grown rapidly in a short period of time. Assimilation was lagging behind. We had just opened up a new entrance that tended to separate people with children from people without children. We had added fifteen or so new staff, more than doubling our previous total, so there was not much community there yet either.

And I was tired. Midlife kind of tired. Church planter tired. Taking it through hotels and elementary schools and high schools and eventually to our land kind of tired. Just built a building, capital campaign, taking it through two expansions kind of tired. Four services a weekend tired.

To add even more gas to the fire, I went for months during this season with an undiagnosed case of whooping cough that was so bad my coughing eventually ended up cracking one of my ribs. I was sick and tired—literally.

So I found myself pulling back, emotionally conserving, and relationally retreating. And as a result my response to the infection was, to the say the least, underwhelming and ineffective. I kept wanting to "win" people and make them like me—which led me to own more of what the ever-spreading dissent was purporting than the truth. The reality was that this was sin, and much of it was sin against me and the church.

But I did not respond the way I should have. If I had, the church would not have lost three years, and I would not have lost three years—and more. I was left so battered and bleeding by the time it ended (when I finally did address what needed to be addressed, or it got addressed for me) that I was ready to quit.

So what should I have done? What *had* I done in the many years leading up to this with success and have followed passionately ever since that has kept such things at bay? Beyond the "Five C's" and hiring from within, I should have met this with zero tolerance. Because that's what it deserved.

I should have fired the person who started it long before I did (and he was eventually let go). I should not have tolerated those select individuals who engaged in parking lot conversations, hallway snipings, "sharing" in small groups, and so much more as they vomited out their own junk. At the earliest of manifestations, there should have been immediate confrontations on the basis of Matthew 18:15 (more on this later), not allowing it to get a foothold in the life and spirit of the church. And those unwilling to be so confronted and brought to repentance should have been removed from their positions and, if need be, brought under church discipline.

Why don't we do this? It's simple. We are by nature pleasers and nonconfrontational. It's like having a toothache but continually avoiding the pain of the dentist's chair. So we live with the ongoing, throbbing ache that grows in its infection until it takes over our bodies in blinding pain—when thirty minutes in a dentist's office would have solved everything.

Go to the dentist.

9

Forever Young

[They] became less formidable when their youth was
drawn away.

Edward Gibbon, *Decline and Fall
of the Roman Empire*[1]

On the list of the many things I never learned in seminary but only discovered from the trenches of actual church leadership is the natural flows of the church that most leaders do not want their church to take. Granted, there are many ways the church will naturally flow in a positive way, and leaders need to learn to get out of the way rather than intercede and mess things up. But there are some natural flows in the church that are the bane of church leaders around the world, and only diligent, interventionist leadership will correct the flow.

One is that the church, left to itself, will naturally turn inward, which is why it takes a disproportionate amount of leadership energy to keep it turned outward. I don't have to spend any effort to get people to have their needs met, take a class they are interested in for spiritual growth, or worship enthusiastically to great music. But it takes enormous effort to get people to die to themselves in order to reach out to others—to not simply invite others to come but to sacrifice themselves in ways necessary for growth, such as attending alternate service times, parking far away, or serving in a costly manner.

Another natural descent involves becoming outdated. Left to itself, the church will find itself frozen in time in terms of decor, style of music, technology, message topics, and methodology.

But the most overlooked, least discussed natural flow—and perhaps the most deadly—is that if left to itself, the church will grow old. Why is this the most deadly? Because if you grow old, it is almost certain you have turned inward and become outdated. And that means you have started the death spiral.

Forever Young

According to data recently released by LifeWay Research, Southern Baptist membership will fall nearly 50 percent by 2050 unless the aging denomination reverses a fifty-year trend and does more to reach out to young adults. According to the director of LifeWay Research, "The difference in the mean age of Southern Baptists versus the U.S. population shows SBC members older, especially since 1993."[2] This is but the latest in a long litany of laments over the aging of the church. Some blame a secular society; some blame traditional approaches to ministry; some blame new forms of individualism that lead Christian young adults away from institutions in general; some blame the lack of evangelism.

Here's the truth: *the natural flow of the church is to skew old.* Left to itself, that is what it will do. It *will* age. You take your hand off of that wheel, and that is what will happen.

I know of one large, innovative church—legendary in leadership circles—that woke up one day and realized that its median age had increased from people in their teens and twenties in the 1970s to the thirties in the 1980s, then the forties in the 1990s, and then the fifties in the new millennium. And this was a church known for its innovation. But innovation wasn't the problem.

I had a wake-up call on this a few years ago. I was asked to speak at one of the fastest-growing churches in the United States, which was made up almost entirely of twentysomethings. The pastor was a former student of mine. I will never forget standing with him, waiting to speak, and watching the band that took the stage, the people who filled the seats, and the staff mingling between the services. I was overwhelmed with one thought of my own church: "We're old." That was hard to accept, because Meck had always been known as the "new" church, the "young" church, the "cutting-edge" church. Now all I could think was that we had become the "old" church.

I went back to Meck the next weekend, and it was as if God wanted to make sure the message had been received. Though it was a bit of a scheduling fluke, every person onstage that weekend—every musician, every singer, every person speaking—was in their forties, except two. They were in their fifties. Though in my forties myself at the time, I was the youngest person on the stage that day. The irony is that we were still young as a church in terms of our attenders—mostly folks in their thirties. But we were losing the twentysomethings, which meant we would soon be losing our thirtysomethings, and on the creep would go.

My goal was never to simply be a church for young people. But the vision was never to be a church for old people either, or to have one generational life cycle before we closed the doors.

Right then and there I made a vow: *we will not die of old age!* If the natural flow of the church is to skew older, then that means the leadership of the church has to invest a disproportionate amount of energy and intentionality in order to maintain a vibrant population of young adults.

So we did. At the time of this writing, Mecklenburg Community Church is now younger than it has ever been in its entire existence, growing faster than it has ever grown, and reaching more unchurched people than ever before.

So what did we do? There are three headlines that are disarmingly simple in maintaining influence and impact with the next generation.

1. *To attract young adults, you have to hire young adults.* It seems simple enough, but it's often overlooked. Very few churches intentionally seek to hire people in their twenties. But without twentysomething staff, you are cut off from the next generation's culture. That includes technology, which is heavily oriented toward new forms of communication. The idea here is the need for reverse mentoring, something that is seldom discussed and much needed.

Case in point: For years, our church offered a periodic "Dialogue Night" during our midweek service. Two or three times a year, I would open up the floor to any and all questions of a spiritual nature that people wanted to ask. These nights were very popular and often provided me with a clear sense of potential future series. After we made the strategic shift away from weekly midweek services and to a monthly "first Wednesday" approach for our core gathering, Dialogue Night was forced to become a once-a-year event. The only way we could offer it more frequently would be to offer it on the weekends, but we had no idea how we could do that with the number of services we had and the size of our crowds.

Some of our younger staff said, "Oh, that's easy. Just have everybody bring their cell phones and text their questions. There is an 'app' that will let us set up a secure number and allow the questions to come to a wireless laptop onstage, where they can be screened. Then the ones chosen can be displayed through the auditorium projectors. We can call it 'Txt ur ?s' weekend. Besides, most people we know would rather text their question than go to a microphone or write it out on a card. It's just easier this way."

Honesty moment: never in a thousand years would I have thought of this. I did not know the technology. I would never have felt "free" to use texting this way, or perhaps better put, I underestimated the freedom and safety others might feel. I loved it. We went with it, and it is now a part of our culture. And the younger folks in attendance? Well, as they say, our church went up a notch in terms of "street cred."

2. *To attract young adults, you have to platform young adults.* One of the unwritten laws of church life is this: who you platform is who you will attract. It doesn't matter whether you want it to be true or not; it simply is. If you want a church of fortysomethings, then be sure to litter your stage with that age group. But don't then sit back and wonder where all the young people are.

Now, before you think you need to raise the banner for the importance of a multigenerational church, I'm with you. But here's another unwritten law: the best way to become multigenerational is to intentionally target young adults.

Here's why. While you can platform older folk and disaffect young adults, you can platform young adults and still attract older folk. Lots of them. A twentysomething person is not attracted to a fifty-year-old man singing a Coldplay song. But a fifty-year-old man *is* often attracted to a youthful, energetic twentysomething person who is singing that song. The stage does not have to be entirely young, by any means, nor necessarily should it, but remember the principle: who you platform is who you will attract, whether young or old, white or black, male or female.

Case in point—I did a blog about this once, and a woman from our church posted the following comment: "I took my eighty-six-year-old grandmother to visit Mecklenburg Community Church on the Sunday that Pastor Jim was wrapping up a series on sex. Grandma *loved* it. And she dug the music. Since she lives right around the corner from Meck, I expect they'll be seeing a lot more of her."

There you have it. You get grandmas with sex and rock 'n' roll. You heard it here first.

3. To attract young adults, you have to acknowledge young adults. To acknowledge a young person is to acknowledge their world, their sensibilities, their technology, their vocabulary, their tastes, their priorities, and their questions. Notice I did not say to *cater* to such things, only to acknowledge them. A church that does nothing but speak to young adults is a glorified youth group and not the vision of the new community detailed in the New Testament. But those who are younger should be acknowledged. Become familiar with their favored musical groups. And by all means, embrace the technology of the next generation, as it will fast become the technology of us all. When using illustrations, don't overlook the world of iPads and Twitter, texting and Facebook. A young woman on our staff commented on hearing a pastor mention in a talk that he was walking while texting and ran into a tree! She said that she knew right then she could identify with him as a person. Why? He was a "texter" like her.

Bottom line? Sometimes bridging a cultural divide is as simple as who you hire, who you platform, and who you acknowledge. Yes, a person who is fifty should come and find points of connection and community at your church. But that's not the problem. We're reaching the fiftysomethings. It's the twentysomethings we're missing.

Don't believe me? Ask a Southern Baptist.

10

Hills to Die On

The kingdom of heaven is like a merchant looking for fine pearls. When he found one of great value, he went away and sold everything he had and bought it.

Matthew 13:45–46

It's an old phrase but a telling one: Which hills are you prepared to die on? Meaning, which stands are you going to take no matter what the cost? For what are you prepared to die? Your answer will determine your core values, and until they are established, your church does not have a defined DNA. And that means it will not be set apart.

If you were to compare the Christian churches in your city by doctrinal statement, there probably wouldn't be much disparity. Most will not veer from the original Nicene Creed established by the early church. If you were to compare them by purpose, again, you wouldn't find too many wavering from evangelism, ministry, discipleship, community, and worship.

We all get cute with nomenclature, but we don't drift far from these five core purposes.

Even comparing your church to other churches in terms of mission won't reveal much to the average observer. The Great Commission is pretty clear; the lesson of the sheep and the goats is apparent. In one form or another, we're going to have a mission that embraces evangelism and discipleship along with social ministry. In a phrase, "the least and the lost."

So what separates churches?

The hills they will die on. Values.

Let me give you our ten core values, and perhaps you'll see what I mean.[1] And here's the lead, just so it's not buried: you need to lay out your core values.

The Bible Is True

Our first value is that we believe that the Bible is true and is the catalyst for change in individuals' lives and in the church. From day one, whenever it comes to what to believe, how to think, how to operate, or where we should land on a particular position or issue, we've had one simple value: go to the Bible, and then go with the Bible. Over and over again, we've just been committed to asking, "What does the Bible say?"

Lost People Matter to God

Our second value is that lost people matter to God, and therefore they ought to matter to us. This value puts us on mission. It tells us we have a clear cause. We are to be turned outward, not inward. Every now and then I get asked how big Meck is going to get. I tell them I have no idea and rarely even think in those terms. All I know is that for us, growth is not an option but an absolute imperative. As long as there is one lost person left in this community, we are going to try to grow.

Culturally Relevant

Our third value is that we believe we should be culturally relevant while remaining doctrinally pure. We are trying to bring the message of Jesus to our world—but not just to our world but to *our* nation, in *our* city, in *our* time. All that means is that what we say and do must make sense to the person *experiencing* it. The apostle Paul had a deep commitment to this, once writing that he became "all things to all men so that by all possible means" he "might save some" (1 Cor. 9:22).

We've always understood this when it comes to foreign missions. Missionaries have learned that when they go out to a foreign country with the gospel, they need to dress like the people, learn the language of the people, translate the Bible into the people's language, and create services that will reach out to their culture.

This value holds that we are *all* missionaries. Our mission field is the United States—and not the United States of a hundred years ago or even ten years ago but the United States of the twenty-first century. And it will take the same kind of effort at meeting the unchurched here on their turf, on their terms, and in their language as it would if we were in the darkest reaches of the Amazon.

Here's the value: the *message* of the gospel is unchanging; the *method* of communicating that gospel *must* change according to the language, culture, and background of the audience. We don't ever want to abuse this or cross a line. The goal is to be in the world, not of it. But we are to be out there on the edge, on the front lines, communicating the gospel in the most compelling, culturally relevant, and understandable way possible. That means musically, visually, stylistically, and experientially. We want to connect through the music people are listening to, the films they're watching, and the books they're reading; we want to meet them where they are and connect with them for Christ.

Spiritually Authentic

A fourth value we hold is our conviction that it is normal for followers of Christ to manifest authenticity and to grow in their spiritual maturity. That simply means that we want to be spiritually real. First, real about our sin. As I often tell our folks, "A sinner has to lead this church, so I might as well be an honest one, or else I just add deceit to my list of sins."

But it's more. It's about becoming more like Christ. We don't view our involvement here like we would a country club. We're not into being one thing on campus and another thing off. We believe that anyone who calls themselves a Christian should be a Christ-follower. They should be authentic in their faith.

That doesn't mean perfection. It doesn't mean Sunday smiles and plastic halos. Authenticity means that not only is our relationship with Christ a real one, but we're going to be real about it. But authenticity doesn't just mean being transparent. It also means *growing*. It's not real if you are the same today as you were two or three years ago. I'm not saying we don't have the same struggles, but there should be progress, growth, development, and maturation. To be authentic means to become increasingly like Jesus.

Servanthood

A fifth value that is dear to us is that the church should operate as a unified community of servants stewarding their spiritual gifts. The Bible teaches that *every* member of the church is a minister—not just the ordained clergy or paid staff of the church. This ministry is to be based, by and large, on how God has gifted them. The Bible teaches that there all kinds of gifts: leadership, administration, teaching, the arts, mercy, counseling, and on and on it goes (I agree with those who read the lists of gifts in Ephesians, Romans, 1 Corinthians, and 1 Peter as indicative, not exhaustive).

We believe that's the way the church should operate. We should have administrators administrating, teachers teaching, singers singing, counselors counseling, and leaders leading. People should discover their gifts, develop them, and be freed up to use them in whatever capacity God intends so that they can make a difference in the world.

But it's not just about gifts or finding a niche. It's bigger than that. This value is about a servant's heart, a servant's mind, and a servant's attitude. It's having a towel draped over our arms, ready and willing to wash any foot that needs washing.

Loving Relationships

A sixth value, one that shapes us on a daily basis, is that loving relationships should permeate every aspect of church life. This value drives me to be a zealous defender of the community of our church. I have been as wounded as anyone, if not more so, by the pain that can be inflicted on people *by* people—particularly within the church. This value simply says, "Not here." Instead, we're going to do everything in our power to relate to one another lovingly, truthfully, compassionately, and graciously.

When there is conflict or tension, stress or misunderstanding, we're going to tackle it head-on within the context of love. We're not going to let it go underground, much less let it become cancerous so that it infects the body of Christ. We're going to pay the high price and do the hard work of community.

I know we won't all be equally close to one another; this isn't about every single person being your best buddy. There may be people you feel a little "allergic" to, but we can still be loving in our spirits, gracious in our hearts, and fiercely loyal to each other.

Life Change through Relationships

A seventh value that we have at Meck is that life change happens best through relationships. We are keenly aware of what other people do for our spiritual life. They challenge us; they push, motivate, influence.

But it's not just challenge. People also bring you the spiritual encouragement you need for life change. We all need people who come along beside us and help us to keep going. We all need people who can put their arms around us and help us make it through those times we cannot stand on our own.

Excellence

Our eighth value is that excellence honors God and inspires people. That's a value for us for two reasons. The first and foremost is because it's the only way to live a life that honors God. God deserves our best. Mediocrity does not honor God, nor does it reflect his character.

But there's a second reason, one that we shouldn't forget. Excellence sends a message. When somebody comes in and sees typos in the program, sloppy printing or mailing, messy floors or grounds, a poorly performed or rehearsed music or drama, or a talk that sounds like it was pulled together the night before, they make a value judgment: "This God you talk about must not be that big of a deal. If he was, you wouldn't do things this way."

So we're passionate about excellence not only because we want to honor God with our lives but also because we know that mediocrity could invalidate everything we want to try to communicate to those around us about Christ.

Let Leaders Lead

Our ninth value is very behind-the-scenes, but it's very, very important and strategic to everything we're about. It's about structure and leadership. We believe that churches should be led by those with leadership gifts and structured according to the nature and mission of the church. This means that we let leaders lead and, further, that we as a church are led by those who have the spiritual gift of leadership.

Not only do we let leaders lead, but we're also structured the way the Bible intimates we should be structured—not with committees and policies and constant business meetings and talk about "who's in control" but along the lines of what a church *is*.

The church is a fellowship, so we structure for unity. The church is a family, so we organize and manage and lead it like a family. The church is a body, so we are made up of people with differing gifts, filling different roles. And the church is a flock, so the church is cared for and led by shepherds.

Full Devotion

Our final value is simple: we believe that full devotion to Christ and his cause is normal for every believer. Not wavering back and forth; not lukewarm; not limp-wristed or halfhearted; not undecided or greeting the whole thing with a yawn.

Fully devoted.

That's what we believe the church demands. As Eugene Peterson paraphrased Ephesians 6:12, "This is no afternoon athletic contest that we'll walk away from and forget about in a couple of hours. This is for keeps, a life-or-death fight to the finish against the Devil and all his angels" (Message).

Now, stating core values is meaningless. Living them, upholding them, modeling them, rewarding them, protecting them—that's what matters. And when that's done, your values become your DNA. So what are your values?

11

Vision Leaks

I was not disobedient to the vision from heaven.

the apostle Paul (Acts 26:19)

One of the most important lessons I have ever learned is that vision leaks. Early on, I thought I just had to have a vision and then, on special occasions, cast it. But my working assumption was that once I cooked it up and served it, the job was done. But in reality, all I had done was create the message that I would be lifting up for the rest of my leadership life.

When I say "vision leaks" (and the phrase is certainly not unique to me), I mean that once people hear it and even "get it," they don't tend to keep it. It burns bright for a season, if you are fortunate, but it tends to fade. It's like a leaky bucket that constantly needs refilling. And it's not just the overarching vision. The values inherent in the vision need their own support, which is why an effective leader is constantly having to talk about such things as serving, giving, inviting, and loving.

And the biggest part that needs constant refueling? The vision of the mission. One of the natural flows of the church is to turn inward; therefore, it takes a disproportionate amount of leadership energy to keep it turned *outward*. I don't have to spend any energy trying to get people to get their felt needs met, to take a class of high value or interest to their spiritual life, or, if they are new to the church, to try out a small group to meet new friends. But when it comes to dying to themselves for someone else—real inconvenience for the sake of reaching someone else—that's an entirely different affair. Then I have to vision cast. And cast, and cast, and cast . . .

If I took my eye off of this ball, within eighteen months we would have people complaining about the music being too loud, about having to park far away or on gravel, that too many people they don't know are coming, and that they can't find a seat. This would soon be followed by phrases such as "I'm not being ministered to," "I'm not being fed," and "I didn't get anything out of it."

But it's important to know not just how vision *leaks* but also the nature of how vision *takes*. I don't repeat things just so the bucket will stay full but so that at some point in time, it eventually takes hold so that I have a bucket to even fill!

One of the lessons I have learned is that about the time I get so sick of saying something that I think I'm going to puke if I say it again and my staff is mouthing the words for me before I even say them—right about that time, the average person sitting in the back risers gets it. I'll talk about lost people mattering to God from Luke 15—for the hundredth time—and some guy who has been attending for years will come up and say, "You know, I think I finally get it!" So it's not just giving ongoing infusions but repetition—saying the same things over and over again. You want to be creative, of course, but not to the point of being afraid of saying what you know you've said before.

Once you realize vision leaks and bears constant repetition, then there are three more things you can do to keep the vision front and center.

Big Church Mentality

Tom Watson was the leader responsible for putting IBM on the map during its heyday. When asked why the company had become so successful, he said:

> IBM is what it is today for three special reasons. The first reason is that, at the very beginning, I had a clear picture of what the company would look like when it was finally done.
>
> The second reason was that once I had that picture, I then asked myself how a company which looked like that would have to act.
>
> The third reason IBM has been so successful was that once I had a picture of how IBM would look when the dream was in place and how such a company would have to act, I then realized that, unless we began to act that way from the very beginning, we would never get there.
>
> In other words, I realized that for IBM to become a great company it would have to act like a great company long before it ever became one.[1]

One of the most important things you can do as a church leader is to establish a preferred vision of the future firmly in your mind and spirit. Then act on it. Make decisions based on it. And most important of all, let people know your thinking.

In the early days at Meck, we used to say that we were "a small church with a big church mentality." We saw ourselves from the beginning as a church of thousands. So we acted like one. When we were running less than a hundred people, we would prepare for each service—in terms of quality, effort, and attention to detail—as if hundreds would come. And that's one of the reasons hundreds did. And then thousands.

It's very easy for a church to act in accordance with its current status. You prepare a service for 250 because, well, that's what you tend to have in attendance. So everything is done with that level of quality, but also that level of decorum.

You do church for 250 people, and it becomes a self-fulfilling prophecy. For a church running 250 to become a church of 500, it has to begin to *act* like one long before it actually *is* one.

Think Globally, Act Locally

But that's not all. As important as it is to have a big church mind-set, you have to have a small act mind-set. You have to help people see how the seemingly small things matter—and specifically the seemingly small things that they are doing. You have to show them why changing a diaper, setting up a chair, rehearsing a song, or writing a check matters. Because it does, but it's not always easy to see.

When you're back in the hot, stuffy nursery watching somebody else's hyperactive kid on a Saturday night at the end of your own long day so that somebody else can sit in the service, it's not always easy to see yourself advancing the kingdom of God.

But say a leader comes up to that person, puts their arm around them, and says, "You know, what you're doing matters. There was a single-parent mom I know of who came to the service tonight for the first time ever, and I think it really impacted her. Thanks for being back here and enabling God to do that in her life. You being here may have altered her eternity."

Suddenly the small thing isn't so small anymore.

January and August

I've learned to get vision on the calendar. Specifically, two pivotal months in the rhythm of the ministry year simply must be seized: January and August. These are the two "get back into the swing of things" months, the two "start of a new season" months that come naturally in the life of your church. January is the start of a new year, and August is the end of the summer and the start of a new school year. Both will see a fresh return of attenders and a sense of "new beginnings."

This means both months are opportune times for vision casting. And not just any aspect of the vision but the three areas where it leaks most rapidly: money, volunteering, and the mission.

I've found that January is the best time to speak to money issues. People are wanting to make resolutions and have a fresh start, and getting financially fit is usually at the top of their list. It's also a time when they are both ready to hear God's instructions and have the means to do something about it. They are ready because they just binged on credit cards for Christmas and are painfully aware of how badly they need to get in shape; they have the means because January is the most common time for new raises to kick in and end-of-year bonuses to arrive. It is the perfect time to help them bring their money under God's leadership and begin experiencing financial freedom.

August is ideal for getting back into things—it's back to school, back to work, and, not to put too fine a point on things, back to church. This makes August a great month to encourage serving and involvement, membership and small groups. It is also a great time to remind people of the mission of the church—what it exists for and why.

It's like the football coach who, at the start of every new season, would stand in front of his team and say, "Gentlemen, this is a football."

Yep, vision can leak that badly.

Put It Out Front

Finally, put your vision out in front of those who just might have the horsepower to make it happen.

The first time I did this, I was prodded by a staff member to consider focusing on a small group of high-octane marketplace leaders with specific projects and needs. I was a bit skeptical but played along. We secured a room at a nearby clubhouse and mapped out a half day together. The essence of the agenda was talking about making a difference with their one and only life and then targeting five or six key dreams that they could own and turn into reality.

I'll never forget one saying yes.

The particular vision was to step into the AIDS pandemic in Africa. An entire generation was being wiped out, leaving millions of orphans in its wake. My heart had been touched to do something, but I knew I needed a leader. I talked about how we could go "an inch wide and a mile deep" or "a mile wide and an inch deep" in terms of focus. I wanted the inch wide and mile deep.

After I pitched it, a man who was then vice president of one of the leading banks in the nation stopped me afterward and said, "I think I could really give a season of my life to that." Within two years our church had partnered with a major relief organization targeting an area outside of Lusaka,

Zambia. We made multiple trips to the region resulting in the sponsorship of over five hundred AIDS orphans, the drilling of water holes, and the establishment of a microeconomic development "bank" for loans for those living in the region.

How? Vision casting.

12

Pick Up the Phone

What we have here is a failure to communicate.

Cool Hand Luke

I saw him at a church conference. He lit up the stage. He was one of the most electric worship leaders I had ever seen. Young, handsome, talented.

I went after him. I had to be a bit discreet—it felt a bit like stealing. He was, after all, serving at another church. But that just added value to his stock, particularly considering the church he was at. So the covert seduction began.

In the end, I got him. I was elated. Buckle your seat belts, church growth world—it's time for warp speed! I had just nabbed the up-and-coming worship leader at one of the nation's most prestigious megachurches.

In less than twenty-four months, he had been removed from ministry and placed under church discipline. He eventually left the ministry, and to the best of my knowledge, he has never served in a church since.

Not long afterward, I interacted with the senior pastor of the church from which I had procured my wunderkind. He graciously asked how my new hire had worked out, and I had to sheepishly tell him that, well, he didn't.

I told him the whole story. After I was done, he said, "I'm not surprised. We had been having issues with him for months. Just before he left, I had entered into some pretty serious conversations with him attempting to confront the very kinds of things you have had to deal with. I was deeply concerned that he went to another church before we could work through anything."

And then he said words that have haunted me and instructed me ever since: "Why didn't you just pick up the phone and call me?"

Good question. Why didn't I? It would have saved me so much grief. I didn't like my answers:

- Because I thought I was pulling off a coup on another church and getting some top-notch talent, and I didn't want my effort botched
- Because I had quietly bought into the idea of other churches being the competition, and this was just the blood and sweat of the contest
- Because I was blinded by the person's talent and never really considered exploring his character the way I should have
- Because I wanted to bottle up that particular church's success and add it to our own
- Because the person in question told me things that were derogatory about the church he was leaving and its leadership and flattered me about the differences my leadership provided in contrast

So I didn't call. And no one calls me either.

I have seen individuals at Meck who were confronted with character issues and subsequently removed from leadership simply flee to another church. Within weeks, they are platformed or placed into leadership. I have seen staff who were within a hairsbreadth of being let go for incompetence quickly leverage Meck's reputation and lobby themselves into a new position at another church.

Why does this happen? Sadly, because other pastors may wrestle with the same dark junk I do. And it's a darkness akin to generational sin, being passed on to others. A single poor staff hire can devastate most churches, squandering kingdom resources and setting back progress for months if not years. And if the issue at hand is sexual, such as someone engaged in serial affairs, then the damage in allowing them to move to another church is unthinkable.

It goes beyond staff, of course. Consider the husband and wife who approach you following the service, telling you how much they enjoyed the service. They inform you that they had been attending another church in the city but go on to tell you how much better your church is—the service, teaching, children's ministry, music, community . . .

By now you are hyperventilating with perverse excitement. "Yes, welcome to our church! We are all the things you noticed and more! Sorry to hear about that other church and pastor. (And yes, I've heard that about them—we have other people here who feel the same way.) Come and enjoy perfection and bliss!"

But in time you find out that the disgruntled ex-member of the church down the street you were so happy to have join becomes the disgruntled ex-member of *your* church now sharing their opinion of you at the church down *your* street that the *next* pastor is only too happy to see them join.

Somebody needs to say it, no matter how uncomfortable, no matter how out of synch it is with the culture of church world: *pastors and leaders of churches, please call the pastors and leaders of other churches.*

When you want to hire one of their staff, call the pastor first. No, they don't want to lose their key players, but most will tend to be honest about those who aren't. And most will also welcome a true God-calling of someone away from their church, knowing that it means God has something in store for them as well. And if they work hard to have the person stay and they stay, well, maybe they were supposed to stay! Let's just openly welcome God into the process and trust him with its outcome.

Call other pastors and leaders when new members come your way—particularly those who spew venom or criticism on their previous church situation—before you fast-track them into leadership or put them on a platform. The other pastor may very well say, "We tried very hard to work with them on some very difficult issues, but in the end, they just fled. The issues remain unresolved. You may be able to serve them and redeem them in ways we could not, but you need to know the cloud under which they left." Or they may simply say, to your relief, "Great folks. Hated to see them go. You've got some real winners there—you should feel comfortable moving forward with them in any way needed."

I know the rules about what you can and cannot say regarding employee reference calls, such as things related to background checks and credit history that cannot be shared. This isn't about violating federal guidelines. Yet the point remains: we must talk to each other.

Why? Because the church *matters*. Not just your church but *every* church. If what we are leading truly is the hope of the world, then let's treat it that way. I think that means it's worth at least a phone call.

13

Spiritually Hazardous

> The place of God in my soul is blank.
>
> Mother Teresa[1]

Let me tell you something you may never have heard before: *ministry is spiritually hazardous to your soul.* If you haven't found that out by now, you will.

Here are some of the reasons why:

First, it is because you are constantly doing "spiritual" things, and it is easy to confuse those things with actually being spiritual. For example, you are constantly studying the Bible in order to prepare a talk. It's easy to confuse this with reading and studying the Bible devotionally for your own soul. You're not.

You are praying—in services, during meetings, at pot-lucks—and it is easy to think you are leading a life of personal, private prayer. You're not.

You are planning worship, leading worship, and attending worship, and it is easy to believe you yourself are actually worshiping. Chances are, you're not.

When you are in ministry, it is easy to confuse doing *things* for God with spending *time* with God; to confuse *activity* with *intimacy*; to mistake the trappings of spirituality for being spiritual.

It's an easy deception. Think about something like the game of golf. I first started playing when I was in graduate school. I took all of two lessons from a course pro, which basically taught me which end of the stick to hold. I bought a cheap set of clubs and began to play. Initially, I made great strides. My score went from the 140s to the 120s, then to the low 100s, and sometimes even the 90s.

Then I'd play the back nine.

But then I began to play with less and less frequency. Soon I only played at the annual Christmas gathering with my wife's family. And as you might expect, I would play about the same each year—translation, horribly—because I hadn't played since the previous year.

It's gotten a little better these days, but it would be very easy to trick myself about the state of my game. Why? Because entering into "golf world" is easy and deceptive. I can subscribe to golf magazines, purchase golf equipment, live by a golf course, wear golf clothing, watch golf on TV, and enjoy eating at the clubhouse—*and feel like I'm a decent golfer!*

But I'm not. That's because simply being exposed to something has little bearing on whether or not we become proficient at it. We can be this way spiritually through our vocations in ministry. Just swap out "church world" for "golf world."

A second reason why ministry is hazardous to your soul is because you are constantly being put on a spiritual pedestal and treated as if you are the fourth member of the Trinity. In truth, your church members have no idea whether you have spent any time alone with God in reflection and prayer over the last six weeks; they do not know what you are viewing online; they do not know whether you treat your wife with tenderness and dignity. They just afford you a high level of spirituality.

Here's where it gets really toxic: you can begin to bask in this spiritual adulation and start to believe your own press. Soon the estimation of others about your spiritual life becomes your own.

This is why most train wrecks in ministry are not as sudden and out of the blue as they seem. Most leaders who end up in a moral ditch were veering off the road for some time. Their empty spiritual life simply became manifest, or caught up with them, or took its toll. You can only run on empty for so long.

I had a defining moment on this in my life when I was around thirty years old. A well-known leader fell—a leader who had been a role model for my life. I was devastated. But more than that, I was scared. If it could happen to *him*, then I was a pushover. It didn't help my anxieties that I was in a spiritual state exactly as I have described: confusing doing things for God and time with God; accepting others' estimation of my spiritual life in a way that made it easy to bypass a true assessment of where I stood. I was like a cut flower that looked good on the outside but would in time wilt dreadfully.

I remember so clearly the awareness that I could fall, that no one would ever own my spiritual life but me, and that I needed to realize that the public side of my life was meaningless—only the private side mattered. This was not flowing from a position of strength; it was flowing from a deep awareness of weakness. So the gun went off.

I began to rise early in the morning for prayer and to read the Bible. I began to take monthly retreats to a bed-and-breakfast in the mountains for a more lengthy immersion in order to read devotional works, pray, experience silence and solitude, and journal. I entered into a two-year, intense mentoring relationship with a man who had many more years on me in terms of age, marriage, and ministry. There was more, but you get the idea: I was going to be a public *and* private worshiper; I was going to be a student of the Bible for my talks *and* for my soul; I was going to pray for others to hear *and* for an audience of one.

I hope you hear my heart on this. It's not to boast; it's to confess. I have to do these things to survive. Maybe you do too. And again, this was not something anyone had warned me about, told me about, or pulled me aside and counseled me about. Interestingly, at the same time my "awakening" occurred, I was part of a breakfast meeting with the great British pastor and author John Stott. He had been touring various American seminaries, and someone asked him for his observations. He did not suggest anything about a diminishing state of orthodoxy, a lack of biblical preaching, or diminished standards of academic excellence. Instead, he said two things that still stand out to me to this day: first, he said he wanted to tell everyone to "cheer up." Seminaries all seemed so serious, so gloomy, so joyless. Coming from a Brit, that was particularly interesting. But second, he said there seemed to be a real lack of spiritual formation—that the seminaries did not seem to be doing much to help people know how to grow spiritually, to care for themselves spiritually, or to develop themselves spiritually. I know it was true for me.

How Much Life Insurance?

But ministry isn't just spiritually hazardous—it's vocationally hazardous too. Your role can keep you from being not only spiritually authentic but also experientially authentic.

You ask people to volunteer, but do you and your family serve in a way that reflects an investment beyond a forty-hour workweek? You ask others to tithe—do you? You lead capital campaigns—would you be at ease if the church knew your pledge? You challenge them to invite their unchurched friends—are you in on that game?

I'm not trying to be antagonistic. These are the questions I ask myself. I just want to make sure that as a life insurance salesperson, I buy it myself. Let me explain.

According to a recent blog by Seth Godin, Zig Ziglar liked to say that with one question, you could tell if someone was a successful life insurance agent: "How much life insurance do you have?"

Godin noted that "If they're not willing to buy it with their own money, how can they honestly persuade someone else to do so?" Godin went on to say, "If you are in the music business but you never buy tickets or downloads, can you really empathize with the people you're selling to?"

His favorite: "If you work for a nonprofit and you don't give money to charity, what exactly are you doing in this job?" "And the shame of it," Godin adds, "is that this inaction on their part keeps them from experiencing the very emotion that they try so hard to sell."[2]

Hmmm. Godin is onto something here, something that runs much deeper than business. Namely, he's identified how easy it is to embrace an ideal, a value, even a mission, and not participate in it yourself; to exhort others to do what you yourself do not—and how impotent it leaves you in achieving whatever it is you most desire to achieve.

For example, I interact with a good number of church leaders, and I am sensing a breakdown precisely along these lines. They attempt to lead a church that reaches the unchurched, and they admonish their folk to reach out to their unchurched friends and invite them to attend, but they could not name a single unchurched person they have personally invited.

They desire to start churches filled with people who will die to themselves for the sake of the kingdom, but neither they nor their family seems to be willing to serve in the bowels of the ministry, whether mopping a floor or tending to a child.

They love to preach and teach but not listen or learn. Or as author and pastor Gordon MacDonald once noted, we can be willing to travel across the country to give a sermon but not walk across the street to hear one.

Result? Ministry becomes little more than a way to create a platform for our own fulfillment and ambition. And then, as Godin insightfully observed, we do not experience the life we so energetically try to sell. And the more that disconnect grows, the less we will succeed.

As I hope I have confessed, I am far from immune to such temptations. So let me put myself into the mix with every other leader and say that for many of us, here's a pivotal question to ask: "How much life insurance do we have?"

14

It's Not Rocket Science

A theory is the more impressive the greater the simplicity of its premises is, the more different kinds of things it relates, and the more extended is its area of applicability.

Albert Einstein[1]

How do you grow a church? Not the way you might think. It is a common myth that "if you build it, they will come." They won't.

Yes, it worked in the movie *Field of Dreams*. A man built a baseball diamond in the middle of a cornfield, to which scores of people came to watch Shoeless Joe Jackson and the 1919 Chicago White Sox. Sounds strange, but it's a fun film.

Sometimes we think that's all there is to building a church, particularly a contemporary church that is designed to appeal to an unchurched person. It's a subtle temptation. We believe that if we offer contemporary dress, Starbucks coffee, and rock music and then deliver a message in a style similar to the popular speakers of the day, we will grow.

No, you won't.

And what's even worse is when the advertising for such efforts, whether through direct mail, radio, or signage, proclaims, "Contemporary music! Casual dress! Coffee!" as if that is what will draw people. People already have those things. They do not need to go to church to find them.

Think of it this way: Today's newspaper probably included dozens of ads for new cars. If you read the paper, did you notice them? It's doubtful—unless you are in the market for a car. Even then, you probably didn't even read the paper but jumped straight to Craigslist or some other site on the internet. So it doesn't matter to you if a dealer is having a sale, promises a rebate, has a radio station broadcasting on-site, hangs out balloons, says they're better than everyone else, promises that they will be different and not harass you or make you bargain over the price, or sends you a brochure or push email. If you are not in the market for a car, it doesn't matter.

It's no different with a church. People today are divorced from seeing it as a need in their life, even when they are open to and interested in spiritual things. They no longer tie that to the need to find a particular faith, much less a particular church.

So how do you grow a church?

It's easy. Really. You know the old line that's thrown out to intimate that something isn't that complicated? "It's not rocket science." That's true for church growth. What it takes to grow a church isn't rocket science.

But *doing it* takes the effort and energy of lifting a rocket off of the ground. In other words, it's not rocket science, but it is hard work. Here's the hard work.

Prayer

You can do a great deal in the flesh—a scary amount, in fact—but truly supernatural breakthroughs come only through prayer. A church grows when its leaders *beg* God for it to grow, when teams gather to *pray* for it to grow, and when members and attenders pray for unchurched people *by name.*

I do not consider myself a good pray-er. I read the stories of someone like George Mueller and sit in awe. Mueller founded and maintained an orphanage in Bristol, England. More than ten thousand orphans were cared for at a cost of millions, and Mueller never asked anyone for anything—anyone other than God. And every time, prayer supplied his needs. But I do pray, and have learned that I must be on guard against making prayer an afterthought. Maybe you've done the same thing I have: you plan carefully, prepare faithfully, and then, at the end, pray for God to bless what you've done. It's better than not praying at all, but it is tacked on at the end. What you do is not *led* by prayer, *born* by prayer, *supported* by prayer. It's not prayer dependent. It's just prayer insured.

Yet church growth is a supernatural event. The Bible's description of the early church is clear: "The Lord added to their number daily those who were being saved" (Acts 2:47). Who added? The *Lord.* Not a program, not a great series, not a tool or technique, not a fast-growing suburb, not the latest hip factor, but the *Lord.*

That means it's a prayer thing.

This is no excuse for passivity, nor am I attempting to speak into various theological debates about just how someone is saved. I'm simply saying that prayer matters. Church growth is a supernatural activity, and we should pray like it.

Partnership

Crawl underneath the hood of any growing church and you will find that the number one reason newcomers attend is because they were invited by a friend. A church grows because its members and attenders talk about it. It comes up in their conversations like the mention of a good movie, a favorite restaurant, or a treasured vacation spot. As Michael Green noted about the explosive growth of the early church, excitement about the gospel and the church is shared like gossip over the backyard fence. In growing churches, this "culture of invitation" is nurtured and affirmed. The attenders of the church are encouraged and unleashed for just this purpose.

I remember an Easter we had gone all out for in terms of attendance, including billboards and mass mailings, all designed to bring attention to the event. We ended up with almost identical numbers from the year before. In a debriefing session, it became clear why—we had focused on telling people *about* the event but not on getting people to invite their friends *to* the event.

There's a difference. You will not grow your church unless your attenders are inviting people—their friends, family, neighbors, co-workers—to attend.

Promotion

You need to market your church. There, I said it.

Before you get your, uh, underthings in a wad, realize that you already do it. Do you have a sign on your lawn with the name of your church and service times? Then you are marketing your church.

Do you have an ad in the newspaper? Yellow pages? A website? You are marketing your church.

The point here is to do it well.

Whether you like it or not, your church has an image in the community. I would have said "brand," but I know that's offensive to many. But that's what it is—a brand. The importance of promotion is about whether or not you are putting forward a positive image. It's about whether the efforts you make for your church and its ministries to be known create a powerful synergy with the invitational efforts of your members and attenders to make inviting easy. At Meck, we've developed a singular logo, a set color scheme, a unique approach to signage throughout the community, key community events, and more—all to establish our presence, and minister, to our city.

Place

In preparation for a building campaign, I visited over a dozen of the fastest-growing churches in the United States. I would fly in, spend an afternoon touring their facility and meeting the pastor (if I didn't already know him) and some of the staff, and then compile my copious notes for our own expansion plans.

At the end of my tour, I compiled my top learnings for our staff. What was it that stood out the most to me about these churches? What was it that seemed to be a common denominator to their growth?

Some were obvious. They had a determined desire to grow. They had simple structures that allowed for quick decisions and flexibility. They were contemporary in their style. But what I wrote at the top of the page was three words: location, location, location.

They didn't just have land—they had land near major interstates or off of major highways. They were on the right side of town in terms of growth.

Let's shoot straight. If you can relocate to a better place, do. If you are not accessible by an interstate or major thoroughfares and won't be in the near future, then you will limit your growth.

If you are going to buy land and can buy fifty acres for your campus instead of five, in most cases you should. If you have five acres, then you will be a five-acre church.

Location, or "place," *matters*. As is often remarked, place is like a shoe, and you don't want the shoe telling the foot how big it can get.

Product

Of all of my "p's," the term "product" for the actual service itself may be the most crass. Sorry.

But we *are* offering something to people. We *are* inviting them to experience, explore, or pursue. My point is not to defend the term as much as to state the obvious: to grow a church, you have to deliver on the service itself. That means well-prepared and well-rehearsed music; a safe, fun children's ministry where kids can learn about God; and a message that is relevant, engaging, and practical (you'll forgive me if I assume the "biblical" part).

Participation

The final component to church is getting people to become participating members—getting them plugged in. I'm not sure of the study behind it, but I've heard it so many times it's become conventional wisdom: if someone doesn't have a handful of relationships within six months or so of attending a church, they will fade out the back door.

Whether there is actually a study backing this up or not, I know from experience that it is true. There needs to be some

Velcro attached to your church that allows people to "stick." The fancy word is *assimilation*. We just call it getting people connected. Whether it's through a ministry or a small group, a seminar or a social event, we want to help people build friendships and a sense of having a "place" in the church as quickly as we can.

Self-Test

Almost every church leader would tell you they want their church to be a growing church—not just in terms of spiritual growth but also numerical growth. Here are fifteen statements that are meant to prod and probe. They are taken from a larger questionnaire I once prepared for our staff that covered the key areas related to church growth we've just discussed.

We gave each statement a response on a scale from 1 to 5, with 1 being "never" and 5 being "always." Any area we gave ourselves less than a 4 was flagged as a high concern in terms of effectively fulfilling our mission. See how you do:

1. You and/or your team regularly pray for the church and your ministry in the church to grow numerically.
2. You are able to pray for unchurched people by name.
3. Members and attenders regularly invite their friends to attend weekend services.
4. There is a high "buzz" factor. Members and attenders regularly talk about the church to others like they would a good movie, restaurant, or vacation spot.
5. Members and attenders believe our weekend services would "win" their friends if they could only get them here.

6. There is a powerful synergy created through appropriate marketing and promotion that makes inviting friends an easy task.
7. Our website is an impressive and effective "front door," constantly updated and user-friendly.
8. Our campus is a warm and welcoming environment from the minute you drive onto the campus until the moment you take your seat.
9. A first-time guest would know exactly which entrance to approach, where to take their kids, where to get information, and where to enter the auditorium.
10. The music is well-performed and well-led.
11. The style of the service, including music, media, and message, is culturally current in ways that allow first-time guests to optimally engage the experience.
12. The messages are relevant, engaging, and practical (let's assume that they are already biblical).
13. The children's ministry is a positive experience for both children and their parents in terms of safety, education, and fun.
14. It is easy for a new attender to meet people and foster new relationships.
15. Our follow-up process to a "surfaced" new attender, whether they came to our attention through first-time donation, first-time children's ministry registration, or information card, is prompt, effective, warm, and impressive.

Did any of these prod you or probe you in a healthy way? They sure did for us.

15

10-10-80

You can't please everyone.

The Paston Letters, 1472[1]

One of the great expectations pastors have is that everyone will like you, and if they don't, they should. When this does not reflect reality, many pastors just redouble their efforts to please as many people as possible. Why?

Many enter ministry with a secret need for approval and affirmation. That's what made them pleasers to begin with. As a result, the goal is to have everyone happy, and even more, happy with *you*.

Get used to disappointment.

The reality is the 10-10-80 principle. Knowing about this principle, and working it to your advantage, is the key to sanity.

What is 10-10-80? Ten percent of the people will instantly take to you. They liked you the minute they met you. They liked your face, your family, the story of your life, and your voice. And they will keep liking you. You could run buck naked through the vestibule and they would say, "Bless his heart, he's just having a hard day." Thank God for such people. You didn't do much to earn their affection, and you don't have to do much to keep it.

Then there are 10 percent who, well, *don't* like you. They didn't like you the minute they met you. They didn't like your face or your voice. Your family may pass muster—as a deacon once proclaimed in the first church I served as pastor, after roasting me publicly in my very first performance review, "Now we all love Susan, of course"—but you do not. No streaking in front of these people. They don't even like the clothes you *do* wear.

Marshall Shelley, longtime editor of *Leadership Journal*, called them "well-intentioned dragons." I'm not sure how well-intentioned they are. But it doesn't matter what we call them; we have to deal with them. It's part of the job.

And like the folk who instantly feel positively toward you, you didn't do much to earn this dislike. It was just there. Your face may have reminded them of someone; something in your makeup threatens them. They liked the pastor before you, and you are the one who took their job. It could be anything or nothing. And there's not a whole lot you can do about it.

This is what is so painfully difficult for a pleaser. They are tormented by the question, "Why don't they like me?" Even more difficult, this 10 percent is often highly vocal and thus the source of stress and opposition, criticism and naysaying. They will often be the thorn in your side, the rock in your shoe, or as I once heard it put so eloquently, the pee in your Wheaties.

That leaves the 80 percent. These are the people who are suspending judgment. They are open to liking you, but they are waiting to see whether you are true to your God, faithful and straightforward in your teaching, honest and caring in your dealings with them, and diligent in your duties. If so, they will happily join the 10 percent who granted you favor without your earning it.

This still leaves the 10 percent who are poorly disposed toward you and your personality. What do you do about them? You must let them go.

Before howls of protest erupt about this lack of pastoral compassion, hear me out. Yes, you are to care for them and pastor them *as they allow you*, but you must not spend your life trying to cater to them and "win them over."

Because chances are, you never will.

Imagine you own a dry cleaning business. Most of your customers are very pleased with your service, and you are growing your company nicely. Then comes a customer who never seems to be pleased. The starch is never right, the fold is never crisp enough, the time of pickup is never to his liking. You give him refund after refund, which only seems to energize him to find even more fault and seek even more concessions, as if your response validates his assessment of your service.

Soon he is taking up inordinate amounts of your time— time that could be spent on finding new, soon-to-be-pleased customers and keeping happy ones happy—and costing you more than he is worth in terms of income due to the number of refunds he demands.

Best advice? Be willing to lose the customer. Serve him well, but stop catering to him. It's better to lose his business than to have him take away time and energy that could be better spent on new and existing customers who are happy—or at least could be.

Are you already shuddering at the thought of applying such marketplace pragmatics to the church? Don't. It's straight from Jesus. When he sent the party of seventy-two out to the surrounding towns and villages, he was quite clear in his instructions: if you do not find the town receptive, move on. Do not waste your time there. Go to a place where your ministry can take root.

Why would this not apply to individuals as well? If you consistently find your ministry is not "taking" with someone, then move on, and allow them to move on as well. Let them find a pastor and church they *do* like. Even more to the point, if you take the energy you are currently spending (or might spend) on the 10 percent who are unhappy with you all the time and spend it on the 80 percent who are suspending judgment, then you will soon have 90 percent of the people happy.

But what if the 10 percent just stay—and stay unhappy? Well, be sure to follow chapter 8, "Zero Tolerance," but here's a word in addition: a 90 percent majority will take care of even the most disgruntled and vocal 10 percent minority. But if you do not take that energy and spend it on the 80 percent who have yet to make up their minds, then that very same 80 percent will be highly vulnerable to the "noise in the system" created by the vocal minority. And soon, instead of 90 percent in your favor, you will be needing to run for cover.

One last thought: sometimes these numbers are off. Sometimes you can find yourself with a very large percentage of people disaffected toward you. For example, if a board brought you in instead of a local favorite, say, the popular youth pastor. Or if the church was traditional and the search team brought you in hoping you'd be a change agent. Or worse, both.

These are terribly unfortunate situations for a pastor. You can be set up to be unpopular. If, after a while, you sense that you don't just have 10 percent aligned against you but far more, then forget everything you've just read. Put down this book, and update your résumé.

Translation: get out while there's still time.

16

We Are They

In dreams begins responsibility.

William Butler Yeats[1]

During my first pastorate, a woman came up to me following a service and said, "I've had a real breakthrough."

It wasn't about my talk. It wasn't even as a *result* of my talk. She told me, "As I was driving away from church last week, I said to my husband that the church really needed to do more with young people in high school. I said, 'They really ought to do something about that.' And then, as soon as the words left my mouth, it hit me. We are they!"

And that opened my eyes to one of the most important tasks of leadership in the life of a pastor: the highlighting of personal responsibility. This is a subtle idea but an important one. Perhaps a quick story will help show what I mean.

One of the most tragic events in American history occurred in New York City in 1964. A young woman from

Queens named Kitty Genovese was stabbed to death. She was chased by an assailant and attacked three times on the street, over the course of half an hour, which in and of itself is tragic enough—but it happened while thirty-eight of her neighbors watched from their windows. During the entire half-hour ordeal, not a single one of them came to her aid.[2]

They didn't run to her aid or come to her rescue.

They didn't shout out or call for help.

They didn't even bother to pick up the phone and call the police.

Shocking, isn't it? It is hard to imagine people acting that way. But we pass it off by saying, "Well, that was a while back, and in New York City. It was obviously a one-time deal. It's not like it's the norm." But that's where we would be wrong.

Situations like that of Kitty Genovese have happened over and over, in cities and towns all over the land. For example, a thirty-year-old mother of six died in Miami, Florida, after she had been brutally attacked. Stabbed and bleeding, she staggered from door to door, pleading for help, near where she had been assaulted—but no one responded to her screams. No doors were opened, no help was offered, no phone was lifted. She collapsed dead in a driveway.[3]

In a book written after the infamous 1964 assault on Kitty Genovese, Abe Rosenthal (who would later become editor of the *New York Times*) offered an explanation for why something like that could happen. And for a long time, what he said made intuitive sense to a lot of people and helped them explain it all away. He said, "Nobody can say [for sure] why the thirty-eight did not lift the phone while Miss Genovese was being attacked . . . [but] it can be assumed . . . that their apathy was . . . almost [certainly] a matter of psychological survival."[4]

What Rosenthal meant was that in a world where you are surrounded by millions of people, with millions of needs and issues and urgencies and cries for help, the only way you can survive is to tune them all out. To become numb. To ignore them. To shut the doors to cries for help. He went on to say that "indifference" can become a "conditioned reflex."[5] We become hard and unfeeling in order to survive. There are too many needs, too many calls for help.

But is that really the answer? Do we just wall up our hearts because there are so many needs out there that jockey for our attention?

Two New York City psychologists—one from Columbia University and the other from NYU—decided that they wanted to dig deeper into what they called the "bystander problem." In a fascinating set of studies, outlined by Malcolm Gladwell in his book *The Tipping Point*, these two psychologists staged a series of emergencies of differing kinds and in different settings in order to see who would come to help.[6]

They found out that one single factor determined whether or not people would respond to a need. It wasn't the severity of the crisis or the degree to which the person screamed or called for help; it wasn't even the characteristics of the people in the experiment—whether they were young or old, male or female, black or white. *What mattered was how many witnesses there were to the event.* The more people who were around, the fewer people tended to respond.

In one of the experiments, they had a student—by himself in a room—stage an epileptic fit. When there was just one person next door, listening, that person rushed to the student's aid 85 percent of the time. But when subjects thought that there were as few as four others who *also* overheard the person having the seizure, they came to the student's aid only 31 percent of the time. From 85 percent response to 31 percent response—just because the sense of personal responsibility had been spread out.

In another experiment, people who saw smoke seeping out from under a doorway would report it 75 percent of the time when they were on their own, but the incident would be reported only 38 percent of the time when they were in a group.

The essence of what the two psychologists discovered is that when people are in a group, responsibility for taking personal action is diffused. It gets watered down. People assume that someone else will make the call, report the problem, or respond to the need. Or they assume that because no one else is acting, the apparent problem—whether it's the sounds of someone having a seizure or smoke coming out from under a door—isn't really a problem, because if it was, others would be responding. Since no one else is responding, there must not be a problem. Or because others are around—witnessing what they are witnessing, experiencing what they are experiencing—the sense of personal duty, of personal responsibility, is somehow lessened.

So in the case of Kitty Genovese, social psychologists argue that the lesson isn't that no one called *despite* the fact that thirty-eight people heard her scream; it's that no one called *because* thirty-eight people heard her scream. If she had been attacked on a lonely street with just one witness, she might have lived.[7] Then that one person might have felt a sense of obligation to respond. They would have been moved by the fact that it really was up to them.

When I read that, a bell went off in my head about leadership. In any large group setting, such as a church, one of the great dangers is the loss of personal, individual responsibility. It becomes almost natural for folks to come, sit, enjoy, benefit, receive, appreciate, and profit but never feel a sense of personal responsibility for responding to the needs within their midst. When they come, it seems like everything is cared for, everything is humming along, and if a need is made known, well, there are so many others around that it never even enters their mind that there won't be a response to meet that need or that things might depend on them.

The idea that they are the key—that what they do or do not do matters—isn't even on their radar screen. It's not because they are hard-hearted and not because they don't care but because they don't feel like they have a personal responsibility to act. They don't have a sense that there is a need for them, and them alone, to respond. They can be lulled into becoming like one of the witnesses to the death of that young woman in New York. People need to be challenged to feel that they have a personal responsibility, and the church has a critical need, for what they do.

Like many churches, we have an electronic system that can flash numbers to alert a parent in a service that their child needs attention. There is also a special number, known to various children's ministry team leaders, that alerts them to an unexpected need for additional volunteers. I remember one weekend when the number was used during a particular service, and so many people came out of the service to help that they had to turn volunteers away. I asked if that was common, and one of our children's ministry leaders said, "Happens every time. People really own the need."

You may think it's a direct reflection of my speaking ability—that people are just looking for a way to escape the service. Perhaps. But whether it's served by my preaching ability or not, it's a value that has to be developed.

When I think about this, my thoughts tend to turn to a story that came out of World War II. A church had a statue of Christ. The church was bombed, and the statue of Christ was damaged. The hands and the feet of Christ were blown off. A soldier came upon it, set it up against a wall, and tried to restore it. But he couldn't.

121

Then a thought came to him, and he stopped trying to repair it and instead wrote a single sentence across the bottom of the statue. On this figure of Christ without hands and feet, he wrote, as if Christ himself were saying the words, "I have no hands but your hands, and no feet but your feet." People need to know that.

17

Bone Structure

Committee: The unwilling picked from the unfit to do the unnecessary.

New York Times[1]

One of my favorite movies is *Paper Moon*. Haven't watched it? You are in for a treat. It portrays Moses and Addie Pray, a father and daughter conning their way through the 1930s American dust bowl and depression. A carnival dancer played by Madeline Kahn manipulates her way into their lives. Young Addie is all tomboy—short hair, overalls, husky voice. Miss Trixie, played by Kahn, is all dresses and curves, hair and having to go to the bathroom every five minutes.

In their climactic moment, Miss Trixie makes it clear that Addie could be pretty. She has what matters most—bone structure. The curves will come, the dresses will come, the men will come. But she has, at her prepubescent best, what matters most—bone structure.

It's true for churches too.

During Meck's early days, we held frequent conferences for church planters. We stopped doing them after a while as we traveled further and further away from our own planting memories and the changing nature of church planting itself. But one thing I told planters then and would tell them now is this: in the midst of all of your dreams for new and innovative services, contemporary worship, great sound and light, and reaching out to new generations of unchurched, do *not* overlook the importance of seizing this one great chance to design your church's structure in a radically biblical form. And whether you have the unique opportunity as a church planter to develop this or not, it is important for any church.

By structure I mean how the church is led, decision-making processes, roles and responsibilities, and general church polity. Church structure may be the single most underrated dynamic of effective church ministry. I've even called it our biggest "secret" to success.

Why? Because church structure either releases the gift of leadership or stymies it. And churches rise and fall on leadership.

I cannot begin to tell you how frustrating it is to lead a seminar or conference, lay out some simple decision or action that would radically improve a church's health or effectiveness, and have it be met by a chorus of leaders saying, "We can't do that." And nine times out of ten, it's not because they don't have the money, or the volunteers, or the facility, or even the desire—it's because they don't have the *freedom*. And if they tried to get the permission needed by whatever authority is in place, they would be shut down because that "authority" is not trained, sensitized, or inclined to make such decisions.

In other words, the ones best able to make decisions are not allowed to, while the ones least qualified are—or decision making is so radically democratized or shared that it can take so much time to act that you lose the window of opportunity!

I know there are a wide variety of approaches to church government, from "elder rule" to a more congregationally based approach. Yet most forms of church government have three features that dominate their structure: committees, policies, and majority rule.

None of these terms can be found in the Bible. And all three can kill you.

For example, committees keep the people who are *doing* the ministry from making the decisions *about* the ministry. Authority and responsibility become separate from one another. An effective structure lets the individuals who are the most intimately involved in a particular ministry, and the best qualified, make the day-in, day-out decisions regarding that ministry.

The problem with policies is what Philip Howard calls the death of common sense. A policy makes decisions and directs procedure independent of the situation. In many ways, this is considered to be the strength of a policy. The dilemma is that it removes *judgment* from the process.

For example, a few years ago the federal government bought hammers using a specification manual that was thirty-three pages long. Why not just trust the person to go out and buy hammers?[2] And if they can't be trusted to do that, then get a different person in the position!

Another problem with policies is that they can become an end unto themselves. Rather than the policies serving the organization, the organization begins to serve the policies. Pretty soon "how things are done" has become far more important than *what* is done.

Here's a great question for your church structure that was first suggested to my thinking by the researcher George Barna:

"Suppose your church had an opportunity to implement a ministry that had a high potential for positive impact, but you needed to get started immediately. Could your church spring into action within hours or, at the most, a few days?" Some of the most strategic decisions we've ever made had to be made within days, if not hours. And we were structured to be able to do it.

Now, about majority rule. Majority rule is rooted in American democracy, and as a result, it has often been incorporated unthinkingly into the church. The first misgiving about majority rule is noted by Yale University professor Marshall Edelson, who writes how an excess of consensus, or an overenthusiasm for democratic principles, can render an organization impotent in terms of actually *doing* anything.[3]

The second misgiving about majority rule, and one far more serious, is that the Bible teaches that the church is a family. In most family structures, the immature (children) outnumber, or at least equal, the mature (parents). In my family we had two parents and four children. If we had voted on everything, we would have had ice cream for dinner every night, never gone to bed, and lived at Disney World.

The church is family, and as a result, it should be understood that its members have differing levels of spiritual maturity. If every decision is made by the majority instead of the most spiritually mature, then there is a very strong chance that the majority could mislead the church.

This is precisely what happened with the Israelites. Moses sent twelve spies into the Promised Land in order to report back to the people if it was everything God promised. All twelve agreed that the land was flowing with milk and honey, but the majority said that the land could not be taken. Only two, Caleb and Joshua, were convinced that God wanted them to possess the land. The people went with the majority, and it kept them out of the Promised Land.

Here's the key to good structure: let leaders lead. I'm not talking about setting anyone up to be autocratic or dictatorial, and there should certainly be appropriate accountability. But don't let that become a euphemism for control. A good structure releases the leadership gift mentioned in Romans 12 as fully as one would allow any other gift to be made manifest.

Ninety Days

I was never more grateful for our church's structure that allowed leaders to lead than when we were forced to leave the high school we were meeting in with just ninety days' notice. We had every door to alternate venues shut, thus forcing us to build something on our recently purchased land.

Yep, we had to build in ninety days. No architectural designs, no civil engineering, no building permits, no capital campaigns.

Ninety days.

I'll never forget standing in front of our church and saying, in essence, "Folks, we've been kicked out. We've got to build—no other venues exist. If you'll follow, I'll lead."

They did. And I was allowed to.

People gave sacrificially of their time and money; they would work all day at their jobs and then head to the church campus to work until the wee hours of the morning. We broke through obstacle after obstacle, coming up time and again against barriers that called for nothing less than a miraculous intervention—and God supplied every single miracle we needed, from the almost instant delivery of steel to the passing of new laws by the Charlotte City Council to allow fast-track building permits.

127

The building was built in ninety days. And each day, decisions were made and courses of action were taken, and all by leaders. No votes, no committees—just truly gifted leaders leading as the Holy Spirit enabled their gift.

How? The structure allowed it.

18

Community
under Construction

The community that speaks a language has learnt it.

Bertrand Russell[1]

Community is not something encountered; it is something constructed. It's built life by life, and the building is often very hard work—particularly because so much of the work involves people who are difficult to work *with*.

Even under the best of conditions, with staff and volunteers you genuinely enjoy great chemistry with, there's no way to be in community with others without friction. It just comes from rubbing shoulders with people. And nowhere are more shoulders rubbed than in the context of ministry.

So how do you get along with others and have them get along with you? How do you not only build community but keep the peace?

Do the 18:15 Thing

By far the most important lesson I have ever learned about relational health is to practice Matthew 18:15. Not just talk about it, not just know about it, but *do* it. The verse is elemental: if you have a problem with someone, go to them and them alone to work it out.

Sounds simple. It's not.

The temptation is to go to six of our friends, telling them our problem and painting the other person as a jerk and ourselves as the victim. Or as John Ortberg once wrote, his tendency is to go to someone else and say, "Let me tell you what's going on here. I just want to lay it out objectively and get some feedback from a neutral third party. Don't you share my concerns about this person, who is my brother in Christ and a deeply disturbed psychopath?"[2]

When you do that, you'll feel better for a little while because you've gotten it off your chest, but all you have done is practiced and then cemented your anger, resentment, or sense of offense and hurt. Ever thought of it that way? You've just practiced your feelings of conflict with this person, drilled them deeper, and put them in concrete. And not only that, you've added to the overall breakdown in community by getting others to be in conflict with the person, to feel what you feel, to be offended like you're offended, to be hurt like you're hurt. Why? Because you've just vomited it all over them. It's a smoke screen for gossip and slander and wider dissension.

Jesus said go to that person and that person alone. It's the only way to contain the conflict and bring it to resolution. That's why I've made Matthew 18:15 a verb. I talk of needing to "do" Matthew 18:15 or to ask someone if they've "done" Matthew 18:15. It also can and should become a leadership value. Someone will go to a person and start talking about a third party—some way they got their feelings hurt or were

130

offended, a decision they disagreed with, or some area where they were disappointed—and if the person they've been talking to has been around Meck for very long, they'll stop them and say, "Hold on—I don't need to hear this. Have you gone to this person?"

Nine times out of ten the answer is no.

Then they'll say, "That's step one. And step two is for me not to hear about it."

Be Quick

Have you noticed how big things get when they're given time to grow? All I have to do is take something home with me, and by the time I see the person in a day or two, it has already gone through a few imaginary conversations in the shower and been magnetized so that every negative thing in my memory—real or imagined—gets attached. When the time comes to actually do Matthew 18:15, my rpm's are way higher than the situation deserves.

So I've learned to be as quick and "on the spot" with things as I can be. I'll be offended or bothered by something, and instead of waiting three days, I'll ask the person for a moment immediately after the meeting where the words were spoken. I'll say, "Listen, I'm sure you didn't mean it this way, but when you said that, it sounded very patronizing." They'll say, "Really? I'm so sorry. I didn't mean anything like that." Then it's done.

So be as immediate and deliberate as you can. There's a reason the Bible says to never let the sun go down on your anger. When the sun goes down, your emotions ramp up.

Watch the Ladder

One of our staff members talked about someone going "down the ladder" one day when they should have been going "up the ladder." What she meant was that a team leader was grip-ing about something to her team of volunteers, and it was totally inappropriate. If the team leader had an issue with something, they should have taken it up with their leader or a member of the staff. And if a staff person has a problem, they should take it up with their supervisor. You take things up the ladder, not down.

There are other ways to watch the ladder. You don't go sideways either. Going sideways means if you are a staff mem-ber, going to another staff person, or if you are a volunteer, going to another volunteer. You must always go up with your concerns; otherwise you are not resolving issues, you are spreading them.

Community is often built not simply on talking things through but on talking in the right direction.

Believe the Best

Another mantra I have learned is to believe the best about those you are in community with, as opposed to assuming the worst. This is not an original perspective, by any means, but I have learned to practice it with greater intentionality than I could have possibly imagined. Why? Because my tendency is the opposite: to instantly question someone's motives, to doubt their intentions, or to be paranoid about their loyalty.

Tied to this is being fiercely loyal to your fellow staff and leaders. You will hear others attempt to tear them down—it comes with the territory. That's when you not only insist that person practice Matthew 18:15, but you also refuse to give whatever it was they tried to plant in your spirit any room to take root.

The heart of believing the best is simply suspending judg-ment in favor of that person. Stephen Covey writes of being on a subway in New York. A man got on with two kids, who promptly began to run wild all over the train. They were yelling, throwing things, pulling people's newspapers down—I mean, they were acting horrible.

Covey asked the man if he wouldn't mind controlling his kids a little bit. The man lifted his gaze as if in a fog and said, "Yeah, you're right. We just came from the hospital where their mother died about an hour ago. I don't know what to think, and I guess they don't know how to handle it either."[3]

Suddenly everything changed in Covey's spirit.

And it should have. But this grace should have been offered on the front end.

Watch Out for Absalom

One last concern, but this one is not for everyone—just for the King David types. David was an incredible, godly, yet flawed leader. I deeply admire him, marvel at his life, and learn significantly from his failures. Most people, if asked to highlight his mistakes, would mention his sexual liaison with Bathsheba.

Fair enough. Just don't leave off Absalom at the gate. Remember that story? Here it is just in case:

> When anyone showed up with a case to bring to the king for a decision, Absalom would call him over and say, "Where do you hail from?"
>
> And the answer would come, "Your servant is from one of the tribes of Israel."
>
> Then Absalom would say, "Look, you've got a strong case; but the king isn't going to listen to you." Then he'd say, "Why doesn't someone make me a judge for this country? Anybody with a case could bring it to me and I'd settle things fair and square." Whenever someone would treat him with special

honor, he'd shrug it off and treat him like an equal, making him feel important. Absalom did this to everyone who came to do business with the king and stole the hearts of everyone in Israel. (2 Sam. 15:2–6 Message)

There you have it. Absalom at the gate, winning the hearts of the people with a hypercommunity, hypersensitive approach coupled with an "I understand and I don't know why David doesn't" mantra. It was simply subversive.

David was a cause-driven man. He had built the kingdom, fought the enemies, passionately worshiped and stood steadfastly by God. But he wasn't the counselor. He wasn't the touchy-feely, in-their-home-eating-pie guy. He was the warrior kind, which made him vulnerable to the Absalom types.

Most leaders are. Which means many of us need to watch out for the Absaloms of the world—or, more to the point, the Absaloms of our world.

Solution? Don't let them get a foothold. Really, I don't know how else to convey this. If you have an Absalom in your midst, don't give them a platform. Instead, marginalize them. Do *not* let them sit at the city gate with access to the people, where all they will do is spread dissent.

Where Will Satan Attack?

Right about now you may be wondering why I'm spending so much time on basic goodwill and healthy interaction. It's because tearing this down is the primary way Satan attempts to attack churches and their leaders. He will do all he can to stir up dissension, conflict, and discord. He will attempt to drive staff teams apart and create animosity among volunteers.

Why? Because he knows that unity is the primary apologetic for a lost and watching world.

Jesus said it would be this unity and this unity alone that would arrest the world's attention and confirm that he was from the Father. We often marvel at the growth of the early church, the explosion of faith in Christ in such numbers and speed that in only a blink of history, the Roman Empire had officially turned from paganism to Christianity. The secret? As Tertullian noted, the awed pagan reaction to the Christian communal life was, "See how they love one another."[4]

That's why it matters.

19

Spiritual Narcissism

To live for the moment is the prevailing passion—to live for yourself.

Christopher Lasch[1]

The names say it all: YouTube. MySpace. And of course, iPod, iTunes, iMac, and iPhone.

If there is a theme to our day, it's that "it's all about me." The technical term is narcissism. In Greek mythology, Narcissus is the character who, upon passing his reflection in the water, becomes so enamored with himself that he devotes the rest of his life to his own reflection. From this we get our term "narcissism," the preoccupation with self.

Narcissism is the classic "I, me, mine" mentality that places personal pleasure and fulfillment at the forefront of concerns. Historian Christopher Lasch went so far as to christen ours "the culture of narcissism," calling it our new religion.

Now, as Christians, this should be antithetical to us. We follow a Savior who said he "did not come to be served, but to serve, and to give his life as a ransom for many" (Matt. 20:28); "If anyone wants to be first, he must be the very last" (Mark 9:35); and "Whoever wants to be great among you must be your servant" (Mark 10:43). And then he bowed in submission to the Father and said, "Not my will, but yours" (Luke 22:42).

Yet our thinking has been invaded by a *spiritual* narcissism where the individual needs and desires of the believer become the center of attention. Have you ever heard the way we talk? "I want to go where I'm fed" or "I need to be ministered to" rolls off our tongues without us even blushing. We walk out of a worship service and say, "I didn't get anything out of it," as if worship is about what we receive rather than what we give to God. And it's killing the church, blinding our vision, paralyzing our mission, and muting our voice.

But is it simply a reflection of a narcissistic culture? Or could it be something we have unknowingly created ourselves?

Consider the first two questions any organization must ask itself (courtesy of management expert Peter Drucker): What is our mission? And who is our customer? The second of these involves crass language, I know, for any church. But let's consider them a moment.

First, what is our mission? I would argue that it is to seek and to save the lost. (How could we have a mission other than the one Christ had and then entrusted to us as the church?) Yes, the Great Commission involves discipleship, but I tire of those who pit evangelism against discipleship, as if doing one prevents concentrating on the other. It's a both-and, not an either-or. But more to the point of the mission, if you never reach anyone for Christ, who exactly will you be discipling? Evangelism must be in the vanguard.

From this comes the second question: Who, then, is our primary customer? It is inescapable: if our mission is to seek and to save (and then disciple) the lost, then our "customer" is the one who is lost. The breakdown is that most churches have a primary focus of reaching and then serving the already convinced. So the mission isn't making disciples but caring for them. From this, services rendered to the believer become paramount. They are the customer in a consumer-driven mission.

That means we are not victims of a culture of narcissism; we are purveyors of it.

Some would say that the place where spiritual narcissism runs amok is in contemporary approaches to outreach that seek to cater to the unchurched—as if such churches are abandoning orthodoxy in any way possible in order to gain warm bodies. Most churches, of course, are doing nothing of the sort. In truth, the real narcissism is among the churches catering to the believer, making their needs paramount. Nowhere does true spiritual narcissism face more opposition than in a church that is choosing to die to itself in order to reach out and serve those around them.

Then it's not about whether you are fed but about whether or not you have learned to feed yourself and, best of all, feed others.

Then it's not about whether you are ministered to but about whether you are, yourself, a minister to others.

Then it's not about whether you got anything out of the service but about whether you gave God anything *of* service.

And that is a church that has died to itself enough to *live*.

It's Not the Church's Job

I love the church. I have given my life to the church. I believe, as is often said, that the church truly is the hope of the world.

138

But we have to make one message very, very clear as leaders: *It's not the church's job.*

Make me close to Jesus!
It's not the church's job.
Save my marriage!
It's not the church's job.
Raise my kids!
It's not the church's job.
Give me friends!
It's not the church's job.
Feed me!
It's not the church's job.

It is not the church's job to give you the life you want or hope for, much less the one that you are expected to forge through a relationship with God through Christ under the direction of the Holy Spirit. The church cannot ensure that all goes well with you. Most of your life is your responsibility.

Why do I say this? To defend the church.

Why do people often come to a church? To get fixed, find friends, renew faith, or strengthen family. That's all well and good, and the church can obviously be of enormous assistance in all four areas. But the church can't be held responsible for these four areas of life, nor should you expect it to be.

Let's try to drive this one home with an example. The parents of a middle school student drop their child off at a middle school ministry. The child does not change into a model Christian student. The parents immediately search for a new church with a more effective middle school ministry.

What is wrong with this picture? What is wrong is the complete absence of any sense that spiritual life is the responsibility of that middle school student, not to mention that spiritual leadership within the family is the responsibility of her parents. Instead, we have a mentality of "drop-off" parenting, which is just part of the mentality of a "drop-off" church. We drop our wives off at a women's ministry to get them to be the wives or mothers we want; we drop our husbands off at a men's Bible study to get them to be spiritual leaders; we drop ourselves off at a service or recovery group to fix our problems or at a Bible study to renew our lukewarm faith.

It reminds me of the sixties and Timothy Leary's famous line regarding not only the benefits of LSD but the spirit of the age: "Turn on. Tune in. Drop out." That is not the way to approach the church.

There comes a time when personal responsibility kicks in. The church exists to coalesce and enrich; to coordinate and inspire; to provide order and leadership. It exists to pull together the collective force and will of those who follow Christ in order to fulfill the Great Commission given it by Jesus himself. Yes, it serves the family trying to raise a child; it seeks to heal those who are broken; it provides the richest of communities for relationships; it offers the necessary resources for a vibrant relationship with Christ. But it cannot circumvent the choices and responsibilities of the human will.

The church cannot do life for someone. That's *their* job.

And one of your jobs is to remind them of it.

20

Don't Preach

People praise me as a "translator," but what I want is to be the founder of a school of "translation." I am nearly forty-seven. Where are my successors? Anyone can learn to do it if they wish. . . . I feel I'm talking rather like a tutor—forgive me. But it is just a technique and I'm desperately anxious to see it widely learned.

C. S. Lewis

Whatever you do, don't preach. I know, you've studied homiletics. You know how to say the word *God* with three syllables. You've practiced the deeper voice that kicks in when you step behind the pulpit.

Lose it.

Lose it all.

Don't preach. Instead, *communicate*.

There's a difference, and there's a very important set of dynamics that makes it happen.

Biblical

First, a good communicator must be biblical. People don't want a self-help pep talk that is merely one person's opinion. People want to know what the Bible has to say.

I know, you expected me to kick this off with something more splashy, but the point is that a good communicator has good content. They offer insights and principles, wisdom and counsel that has real, transcendent value. You don't have that in and of yourself—at least not much. Neither do I. But we have *the* owner's manual for life. The more you use it, the more people will listen.

Relevant

The second step in communicating is relevance. I know the word is tired, and it is often a whipping boy for those who feel that contemporary communicators are swapping relevance for orthodoxy. Don't let that sidetrack you. Being relevant has nothing to do with watering down the truth of the gospel. It has nothing to do with removing all references to sin, the cross, or commitment. It does not mean having to stay with topical messages that deal solely with issues such as parenting, family, marriage, self-image, and rela-tionships. All I'm suggesting is to avoid giving a nineteenth- or twentieth-century message to a twenty-first-century audience.

There are three ways a message should be relevant. The first has to do with your sermon topics. They really should address people's life issues and questions about the faith. That doesn't mean that you only talk about what they want you to talk about—they don't know that they need the whole counsel of God brought to bear on their life. But it does mean that you try to bring as much of the counsel of God as you can to them through the door of their interests.

But this is about more than just raising their questions and answering them; it's also about talking about those questions in ways that make it clear to the seeker that you understand the question and you appreciate the issue. Otherwise you'll simply be dismissed as not understanding life as it's lived in the real world.

A second area for relevance has to do with your sermon illustrations. Your stories, anecdotes, quotes, and analogies need to be as fresh and current as possible. If you're going to reference a movie, make it a recent one; if you're going to reference a TV show, make it one that's hot now. Keep on top of current events and cultural happenings.

I remember talking to a young student at a nearby university who attended our church shortly after we planted it, in the early to mid nineties. She was not a Christian at the time, but a friend had invited her to attend. When I was dialoguing with her after a service one day, she complimented me on my talk. She said that the one and only other time she had attended a church was with her grandparents, and the pastor was continually using illustrations from the sitcom *All in the Family*. She said it never connected.

That makes sense—she'd never seen the show! *All in the Family* was an Emmy Award–winning sitcom that introduced the world to the classic character of Archie Bunker, but it ran between 1971 and 1979. When it went off the air, she would have been maybe five years old. Suffice it to say, television had moved on. That pastor's illustrations should have too.

Finally, use language and terms that are relevant. The English language is constantly evolving and changing, and the words we use to express ourselves are constantly changing. I don't think we should try to be trendy or faddish; just try to talk and explain things in ways that people can understand, using analogies and phrases and vocabulary that they can relate to. Put what you say in their language, in their terms, on their turf. Too many pastors speak in ways that they don't communicate in real life.

Practical

A third mark of a communicator is that they are practical. For a talk to be practical means that the listener can apply it or use it; they can work it into their life. One of the best ways you can do this is to make your sermon points your application statements. Rather than give a talk on three reasons you *should* be a better husband, have your message be organized around three steps toward *becoming* a better husband—see the difference?

If you intentionally turn your sermon points into your application statements, you'll transform the message into a practical one. Not every message should follow that format, but it's a great way to get started.

Credible

One of the least talked about characteristics of a good communicator is that they are credible. You have to be *believed* to be *heard*. So how do you gain credibility?

The first has to do with *accuracy*. Nothing blows your credibility faster than engaging in what I have come to call the "misses"—*mis*pronouncing a word, *mis*quoting a source, or *mis*representing a perspective. Early on in my ministry at Meck, I gave an illustration that referenced the Mackinac Bridge in Michigan. I had never crossed the bridge myself, but I read a great story about it. When I told it, I pronounced it the way it is written—with a hard *c* at the end. That is not how it is pronounced. It's actually pronounced "Mackinaw." Immediately after our Saturday night service, a first-time guest who had just moved from Michigan came up and corrected me. And then when they got done, a second person, also from Michigan, stopped to correct me.

Once is helpful; twice is annoying. But I really was glad—particularly that it happened on a Saturday night and protected me from repeating it throughout the Sunday morning schedule of services.

It also taught me a valuable lesson: to double-check *everything*. When you *are* accurate, enormous credibility can be developed.

After I gave a talk on homosexuality, a lesbian seeker who had been attending our church stopped me and said, "I knew what you were going to say. I just didn't know how you were going to say it. It was fair, and you gave me something to think about." In fact, she bought several copies of the message to give to her friends. Her line of thinking intrigued me, because her starting point was accuracy: Is he going to distort homosexuality and the homosexual life? By avoiding stereotypes and caricature, I earned the right to speak to her about my understanding of the Bible's perspective on homosexuality.

Attention to accuracy will serve you well beyond the immediate topic. When my lesbian friend listens to me talk about other subjects, such as the issue of salvation and eternity, she will probably have greater trust in me. I was found to be accurate in an area where she had firsthand knowledge, which was a good sign to her that I just might do my homework on other topics and can be trusted there as well.

Another important area that is crucial in regard to building and maintaining credibility is the practice of personal integrity. No speaker can effectively model the entire body of Christian truth with perfection, but if the gulf is too wide between word and deed, then credibility is at risk.

If people know I am committed to my family and I have raised my kids in a way that has produced godliness and character, they listen to me more intently about parenting. If they know I live within my means and have managed my money well, they listen to me about money with more openness.

Credibility is found in doing what we say we're going to do—and being who we say we are. There's an old line that says, "Who you are speaks so loudly, I cannot hear what you say." We could adjust it a bit to read, "Who you *aren't* speaks so loudly, I cannot hear what you say."

Tell Stories

A fifth mark of a good communicator is that they use stories, pictures, images, props, or media to help convey their points.

I'll never forget hearing a speech on child abuse. A young woman walked out onstage with a single rose in her hand. Without saying a word, she held the rose up in one hand, and with the other she crushed it and then let the petals fall to the floor in disarray.

Then she broke the silence: "That's what child abuse does to a child."

I still remember it to this day.

People think visually, and they craft their thought in terms of images. So when I tell a story, I try to make it a visual one—one that conjures up a picture in their mind. Or I just go for the picture itself: instead of telling a story, I'll just go to a clip from a movie or use a prop that I've brought out onstage. As one woman said to me about a prop I had brought out onstage for a talk, "I didn't know what it was for—but just having it out there intrigued me, and the whole time you were talking I was engaged, trying to think how you were going to use it."

Dialogue

Another mark of messages that truly communicate is that they embrace a sense of dialogue. It's not necessarily literal dialogue but a sense that you know there is an audience out there listening that is thinking about what you are saying and might just have a question or two.

A good communicator will pause every now and then and say, "Now, right about now you're probably thinking . . ." or "If you're like most people, this instantly raises the question of . . ." or "Ever felt like that? Me too!"

This way you create a sense of narrative that they can identify with and find themselves in. I believe it was Arthur Miller, who wrote such plays as *The Crucible* and *Death of a Salesman*, who said that success for him is when someone could sit in the audience, watch one of his plays, and say, "That's me up there."

Be Authentic

A final mark is that you are authentic. Authenticity is no more—and no less—than being a person who can be believed, accepted, trusted, and relied upon to be *that which is as presented*.

I talked with a woman in our church who had been unchurched for seventeen years before coming to Meck. I asked her what it was about our team of communicators that had impacted her. I was surprised that she did not even have to pause. She said, "I never felt 'preached to.' Instead I felt 'talked to.' I could identify with you as people. You shared your struggles, your life experiences, in a way that I could relate to. You didn't come pretending to have your act together, talking down to everybody."

Authenticity is when a speaker is willing to share who they really are, without masks or pretension. I'm not talking about being maudlin or having little or no discretion in terms of revealing your personal life. The key is to be authentic, which means to be *real*.

People in your audience know that you have junk in your life; they're just waiting to see if you'll own up to it. Many of us were taught to withhold our true selves from those we serve. The idea was that if the realities of our life became known, we would lose our moral influence and ability to provide spiritual leadership. In actuality, the opposite is true.

A man who drank too much, got behind the wheel, and killed a young mother by crossing the median strip is much more effective on the subject of "Don't drink and drive" than the average police officer. A person who has struggled in a difficult marriage and remained committed is much more winsome and compelling than someone who proclaims, "We've never had an argument."

So share when you have screwed up more than when you were the hero. And share where you have lifelong struggles. I know this is tough, but it can be so helpful to others. Most folks at Meck know that I've struggled with relationships and community. I never had much of it growing up, and my personality struggles with intimacy and openness beyond my family and a close circle of friends. Letting my listeners know this is one of my "areas" brings an honesty to my speaking.

Authenticity does something else too: it gives the listener permission to be authentic. When we are open and authentic about *our* lives, it allows those to whom we minister to be open and honest about *their* lives. Deeper ministry begins

148

when you can create a context where people can stand up and say, "My name is John, and I'm addicted to porn"; "My name is Betty, and I have breast cancer"; "My name is Steve, and my marriage is falling apart"; "My name is Bill, and I have AIDS"; "My name is Carol, and I just lost my job"; "My name is Alice, and I'm lonely."

When this happens, we open the door to the giving and receiving of both grace and truth. And isn't that what we're trying to accomplish as communicators?

One final point: Want to know the best way to learn to communicate? It's easy. Listen to great communicators. Identify five or six speakers you sense know what they're doing, and go to school on them. Listen to how they manage material, how they open and close their talks, how they admonish and confess.

Remember, those who can, do. Those who can't have never listened to those who can.

21

Safe People

During the time he was in Jerusalem, those days of the
Passover Feast, many people noticed the signs he was
displaying and, seeing they pointed straight to God,
entrusted their lives to him. But Jesus didn't entrust his
life to them. He knew them inside and out, knew how
untrustworthy they were. He didn't need any help in
seeing right through them.

John 2:23–25 Message

Shortly after we started Meck, a man arrived who had a
strong, outgoing personality and eagerly championed the
vision of the church, as he'd been been involved with a similar
community of faith in another city. He was willing to serve, had
previous experience, and understood the vision. He even tithed!
What wasn't to like? I quickly began to lean on him and count
him as a friend. I needed one too—someone I could share the
ups and downs of church planting with. A real brother in arms.

But as the church grew and other leaders took responsibility, decisions were made and teams were formed without his involvement. Instead of welcoming the vitality, he became threatened and turned hostile, particularly toward me.

I vividly recall the day things exploded. We had just moved into our very first office, a small suite with two rooms and a work area. This man had gone in and arranged the furniture as he thought it ought to be. I assumed he was just being nice, but as it turned out, that was his way of marking his territory as the church moved into a new era.

Other leaders came to me and said, "What do we do? We appreciate his efforts, and we don't want to hurt his feelings, but we want to arrange our furniture our own way."

In a blazing moment of naïveté, I said, "I'm sure he won't mind. Go ahead!" Two days later, we made one of our first major purchases as a church—a copier. And we rearranged the office back to the way it was when we first moved in.

When this man saw that we had reorganized the office *and* made a major purchase without his knowledge, he was not happy. His attitude took a major turn, and I didn't have the ministerial street savvy to see it coming. To add fuel to the fire, over the next few weeks we put together a management team that did not include him (we had begun to see some red flags in his personality). When that happened, it was "game over." He went on the warpath.

Where I was once the one he was eager to support, I now could do nothing to please him. He began talking to anyone who would listen, spreading all kinds of innuendo. I tried to talk with him and reconcile, but he would not be appeased. He was mad and wanted others to know he was upset.

The turmoil went on for two or three months. Finally, when he realized he wasn't succeeding in getting other people to revolt, he left. But not before writing a scathing letter to everyone on the management team, accusing me of being loose with the church's money (the copier) and of being autocratic (establishing the management team without him on it).

I tried to talk with him in person, but he refused to meet with me. So I wrote him a letter trying to explain my decisions. All that did was generate another round of angry letters sent to other people. So I just let it go, and let him go, and tried to move on. But you don't just move on from those things. I had trusted this man, confided in him, believed him to be safe. He wasn't.

About that time, I talked to another pastor in another state. He told me about his new church and how, in his efforts to solidify the structure, a woman who had been part of the founding core was not invited to be part of the new leadership team. The woman went on the warpath against the pastor and sent letters to everyone in the church accusing the pastor of financial wrongdoing and of being autocratic and dictatorial. When I heard that, I thought to myself, *Is there a school where they train people for this?*

Nothing hurts more than someone you thought was a friend becoming a foe and attacking you personally. Little did I know that in ministry I could look forward to many more relational defections.

So can pastors have friends? Safe ones?

Some say no, at least not within the church. Some say yes and that building intimate friendships from within the community you are charged to lead is decisive.

I'm not in either camp. I think you *can* have friends within the church you lead, but they are to be few and far between. I don't mean "small *f*" friends, people who are more than acquaintances but less than lifelong intimates. But for a "capital *F*" friend, someone you really do life with, open up to, become vulnerable to, and share your fears and insecurities, secrets and struggles with . . . you are probably going to have to go somewhere else. And you probably should, because most of the people in your church are not going to be safe for you.

It's not the church's fault. You simply have a role with them that makes the relationship weird. I often joke that being a pastor is like being of a third sex. People aren't normal around us. They have ridiculous expectations; they build up and then tear down; they are fans one minute and foes the next. We're just so . . . high-voltage. It's hard for people to interact with us without great risk.

Pastors really are vulnerable here. We lead lonely, isolated lives. We want community, but it's difficult to participate in it. Don't get me wrong—the vast majority of the people in our church genuinely love and appreciate us and would never consider themselves unsafe. And as normal people to normal people, they aren't. But we aren't normal. The nature of our role makes things toxic. Someone wants us to let our hair down around them—even encourages it, saying that they want to be that kind of friend to us, knowing that pastors probably don't have too many friends like that—but somewhere inside of them is an expectation, like a time bomb waiting to go off. All it takes is one disappointment, one failure, one letdown, and all bets are off. Sadly, it's often the ones who most invite you to let down your guard who prove most likely to betray you.

So what do you do as a pastor? Get savvy about people. Have friends, but be careful. And that begins by knowing what makes someone safe.

A safe person is someone who is just that—*safe*. They can be trusted. They are accepting and supportive. They let us love and be loved. Then there are unsafe people. Unsafe people abandon, take advantage, betray, misunderstand, and even attack.

Jesus certainly employed this kind of discernment. Look at how the Bible talks about this aspect of his life:

> During the time he was in Jerusalem, those days of the Passover Feast, many people noticed the signs he was displaying and, seeing they pointed straight to God, entrusted their lives to him. But Jesus didn't entrust his life to them. He knew them inside and out, knew how untrustworthy they were. He didn't need any help in seeing right through them. (John 2:23–25 Message)

Jesus was not closed to the risk of intimacy, because we know that he was in intimate community with several men and women. But here we learn that he never approached relationships with reckless abandon. He approached people lovingly but with a discerning spirit.

So how do you do that? It begins with determining whether they have the maturity to separate your role from who you are as a person. Believe me, this takes a very special person. They need to be truly, truly safe. That means safe with your sin, because that's the key. You are a sinner, and those closest to you will know it—and when, where, and how. Can they show you the grace you need, the grace every human needs—even those of a third sex?

Henry Cloud and John Townsend, a pair of Christian clinical psychologists, put together a useful list of what marks unsafe people.[1] Notice how many of these marks have to do with gracelessness:

- An unsafe person thinks they "have it all together" instead of being willing to readily admit their weaknesses.
- They tend to attack, criticize, and fault-find instead of build up and encourage. They're often legalistic, rigid, and lacking in grace. They are more concerned with making corrections than making connections.

- They're abandoners, with a track record of starting relationships but never finishing them. They look for perfect people, and when someone shows imperfection, they move on.
- They're defensive instead of open to feedback.
- They're self-righteous instead of humble.
- They're unstable over time instead of consistent. They're flashy, intensive, addictive types, going from thing to thing, place to place, person to person.
- They are more concerned about "I" than "we."
- They resist freedom instead of encouraging it.
- They condemn us instead of forgive us.
- They gossip instead of keeping secrets.

When you see some of these marks in someone's life, be careful. Obviously, no one is perfect. Don't forget—you're supposed to be safe right back at these folks. All of us have flaws in our character. No one is completely safe. But that doesn't mean you don't take a deep look at someone's relational makeup and make some assessments about that person before you plunge headlong into a relationship.

Jesus sure did.

22

PKs

Sons are a heritage from the LORD, children a reward
from him.

Psalm 127:3

I am the father of four children. They're all pretty much
grown now. Two are married, and two are in college. They
grew up in the church as part of that infamous fraternity
known as "PKs" (pastor's kids). Many assume they must
have been rebellious and resentful of their role and are now
fiercely anti-church and perhaps even antagonistic toward
Christianity itself.

At the time of this writing, my oldest daughter is the director of children's programming at a church in St. Louis while
her husband completes medical school; my youngest daughter
and her husband are in seminary preparing to plant a church;
my oldest son interns at the church I lead and wants to invest
in children's ministry upon graduation; my youngest son is a

member of our worship team and wants to be a pastor one day. They love Christ, love the church, and love the church they grew up in with their father as their pastor. How?

Don't worry—I'm not about to try to offer a sweeping parenting essay, much less try to convey my top parenting principles. You've done your own share of sermons on the topic. But there are a few things unique to parenting as a minister that I will offer, things that now, looking back, my wife and I see as decisive for our kids surviving their fishbowl existence as PKs—and even more, loving the church they were raised in.

They Never Knew

First, they never knew they were PKs, because we never treated them that way (or allowed anyone else to either).

It reminds me of a story I once read of a teenager who had a large and disfiguring birthmark over much of his face. It didn't seem to bother him in the slightest. He was well liked, his self-image seemed secure, and he didn't seem self-conscious in the slightest.

Someone once asked him about it and why it didn't seem to bother him. He said, "When I was very young, my father started telling me that the birthmark was there for two reasons: one, it was where an angel kissed me; two, the angel had done that so my father could always find me easily in a crowd. My dad told me this so many times with so much love that I actually began to feel sorry for the other kids who weren't kissed by the angel like I was."[1]

That's the way we raised our kids in relation to their "birthmark" as PKs. We never told them that because their parents were in ministry they had to act a certain way or go to certain events. We never made it a liability or a weight they had to carry. We tried to make it something wonderful, a privilege and a perk that others didn't have.

I really believe this is important. My kids knew Daddy was a pastor, but that only meant that they were "special." It meant that people knew who they were, loved them, and cared about them. For them, it simply meant a large, extended family.

We Served Together

Another dynamic that was critical is that we served together as a family. In the early days, when the church was being planted, we would go to the elementary school on Saturday mornings and mop, vacuum, place chairs, and set up nurseries. I would go by the local doughnut store and load up on doughnut holes as a treat for them and the other volunteers, and then we would work as a family. We would laugh, play, and horse around. We made "church work" *family* time, and the kids learned to look forward to it. They associated going to church with pleasure.

This set a precedent for the ensuing years, as together we continued to serve in the church. Some of our fondest memories as a family were loading up on Saturdays as Susan would go early to set up the children's ministry with our oldest daughter, Rebecca; my sons Jonathan and Zach would work with the facilities team as the campus prepared to welcome the first of multiple services; my youngest daughter, Rachel, would be rehearsing with the band as a vocalist; and I would be doing my own preparation for the first of several talks.

We arrived as a team and together had a sense of ownership and investment. There was joy in serving together and then talking afterward about people we had met, stories we had heard, and increased crowds we had witnessed. We had community as a family but then entered the community of the church *as* a family. Our kids were so deeply involved that they felt it was *their* church as much as I did.

Gifts and Passions

Another dynamic of parenting that we were deeply committed to was allowing each of our children to discover, and then chase, their individual gifts and passions. Rebecca was the creative programmer and up-front personality; Rachel was the artsy songstress; Jonathan was off-the-charts gifted with children and children's programming; Zach was the writer, musician, and thespian.

Each was encouraged to chase their gift in the life of the church, and I ensured that they were able to (as I would have enabled anyone else). So the church became the place for them to express themselves, spread their wings, take bold steps, and even take a few risks.

No Command Performances

One of the more important decisions we made was letting our kids interact with the church's offerings like any other set of kids. As mentioned earlier, we had no command performances for our kids, even in the one area where you would think there *had* to be, which was student ministry. We took a bit of heat for that one early on, but we were fully prepared to stand by our decision. We knew the fishbowl our kids could have experienced and the expectations that could be placed on them—be here, do that, attend this. We also knew that such a regimen could create not only burnout but resentment.

So we decided early on we were not going to make our kids do anything other than attend the weekend services and accompanying children's ministry, and not even that as they got older. Some of my kids were heavily involved with middle school and high school programs; some were not. They were already in church so much, attended a private Christian high school (which was like one great big student ministry effort), and were so heavily involved in serving in other areas that we just didn't have it in our hearts to ask them to do more.

It was the best decision we ever made. We felt that the more things were commanded, the more they would be resented.

Protect the Home

One of the banes of ministry life is the evening meeting. It wasn't for our family. To protect the home and particularly the evenings was paramount to me. Fellow pastors are shocked at how rarely I have any kind of evening engagement. Apart from evening services, I can count on one hand the number I have allowed to enter my life. The evenings are simply family and home time, and they deserve to be kept that way.

You may think, "Then when do you meet with the lay leaders of the church?" Easy—over breakfast or lunch. And they prefer it that way, because they want to be home with their family too!

One Last Value

I've given you some thoughts on raising kids as a pastor. It's not an exhaustive list nor a perfect list. But it is a *practical* one.

One final thought—actually, I suppose it is a guiding value. Some of you may not agree with it. That's fine. But I stand by it.

My family took precedence over the church.

I have no doubt that Meck would be much bigger today if I had prioritized it over my children. I have no doubt that I would have a bigger staff, a bigger budget, and a bigger attendance.

I am so glad I don't. If I had put the church above family, I might have had a bigger church, but I would have been less not only as a father but also as a pastor.

That sounds counterintuitive, but the Bible says one of the prime qualifications of a pastor is to be a good father to your children. If a pastor doesn't care for his family, how can he care for the family of the church? The idea is that it's basically the same skill set. If I had cut corners with my family at home, you can count on the fact that I probably would have cut corners on my family at church. Bigger? Maybe. Better? Doubtful.

I recall one time I made a very big decision related to a ministry commitment for the sake of my family. It involved a very important position. I didn't know it on the front end, but after a year, it became very clear that what was being asked for from that ministry would be highly detrimental to my children. I resigned from that position.

I recall a board member standing up, angry at me for my decision, and saying, "I want to know where in the Bible it says that your family comes before your ministry! What happened to sacrifice? To commitment?" Another told me I was committing career suicide.

I was so floored I was almost speechless. I know now what I wish I would have said: "My commitment to my family was made long before my commitment to this role. I am a father first and a leader second. The Bible makes that commitment a prerequisite to even *serving* in ministry. How many men look back on lives spent in ministry, only to see children who are far from Christ, with vacant, bitter hearts, because of an absentee father? You can get any number of people to lead this institution. I am the only father my children will ever have. God has placed me in that role before any and all others. My commitments begin with Christ, but then Christ calls me to be committed to my wife and to my family. My ministry is a distant third. You are right—I am called to sacrifice. And I will gladly sacrifice myself, but not them."

Now, years later, I can tell you that it was the best decision I ever made.

23

What a Leader Does

If God has given you leadership ability, take the responsibility seriously.

Romans 12:8 NLT

What is it, exactly, that a leader does? We are bombarded with directives to be leaders and to lead our church, and we're told that everything rises and falls on leadership . . . okay, what does that actually mean? I was once challenged to pull together a description of what being a leader actually involves on a day-in, day-out basis. I found it to be an intriguing exercise, because in truth, most leadership books talk about how to do certain leadership functions well but rarely lay out the leadership menu. Here's the menu.

Casts a Compelling Vision

The first thing a leader does is to cast a compelling vision. It's seeing all that could be and should be and painting that picture clearly enough for others to get there. We talked about this under "Vision Leaks," so let's move on.

Draws Others In

Second, a leader draws people in. Have you heard of something called the "art of the ask"? The art of the ask is seeing someone and envisioning what they can become—imagining what they can do with their life, spotting their talents and abilities—and then asking them to put their life into play for Christ.

Most people would never see themselves doing anything in ministry—they need someone to believe in them, challenge them, see their potential, and encourage them to give it a try. I could tell you story after story of people who were on the sidelines but in truth were just one challenge away from experiencing what God could do with them.

"I think you could be a small group leader." "I think you could head up a building team." "I think you could oversee a media ministry." "I think you could do some drama." "I think you could sing." These are the words a leader offers.

Think of it this way: If someone handed you a million-dollar check, would you know how to spend it? Would you know how to dream about it? Sure you would. Think of people as million-dollar checks, and dream about how they could be used. Then ask them to write out their check.

Establishes and Upholds Values

A third thing that a leader does is to establish and uphold values. As discussed in an earlier chapter, at Meck we have ten major macro values. They need to be upheld, modeled, championed, and defended.

But there are also micro values. For children's ministry, it might be arriving on time or calling in if you can't make it. For a small group leader, it might be the "empty chair," meaning that there is always a place—and a desire—for someone new to join. For someone in student ministry, it might be never letting a kid get excluded from the group.

When it comes to values, a leader does two things: first, a leader establishes them. That means that you put them into place; you teach them. But it's more than that—you model them.

Let's say I ask you to build relationships with the un-churched. If I don't do it myself, I have no credibility. If we ask people to have a positive attitude, but we don't, we lose credibility. You never lead from title or position but from moral authority. There's an old line I'm sure you've heard: "speed of the leader, speed of the pack." It's true.

But after you establish the values through word and deed, you have to uphold them. This means you catch people living by them, and you praise them and make them an example to others. It also means that when someone plays fast and loose with one, it's lovingly but firmly confronted. I know, we're afraid of offending people. But the biggest loss of volunteers comes when a leader *doesn't* take their ministry seriously. When the bar isn't raised, people tend to blow it off—and their attitude and spirit spreads.

In one of my favorite sports movies, *Remember the Titans*, which explored the dynamics of race through a high school football team in 1971, the young white captain approaches his black coach and asks to cut his best friend from the team for failing to block for the black running back. Reflecting on all he had learned through training camp, he said, "Sometimes you just have to cut a man."

He was right. Sometimes you do. For the sake of the team.

Brings Everything into Alignment

A fourth thing that a leader does is to bring everything into alignment. This is often talked about in business circles but less so in church circles.

Alignment is translating values, purpose, mission, and goals into the very fabric of what you are trying to do on a day-in, day-out basis. It's having *what* you do line up with what you *say* you're trying to do. It's having every little decision informed by the big picture of what you're trying to accomplish. Alignment is what lets a leader make a decision—to know what to say yes to and what to say no to. It helps us think creatively about what to start, what to stop, what to create, what to change, what to continue, and where we need to experiment or innovate.

On a practical basis, this plays itself out in at least three ways. The first is how you use people. They should be aligned with their gifts and strengths but then pointed toward those things that will further the mission. The second has to do with resources. The reality is that you have a finite amount of resources, such as money; alignment means that it goes toward those things that achieve your goals. The third has to do with events and activities. There are a thousand things you can do; alignment means that you are tenacious in doing those things that will further the cause.

Lets Others Play in the Game

Fifth, a leader lets others play in the game. At the most basic level, this is just learning how to delegate, which surprisingly few people ever really learn to do. The key to delegation is simple: Do only what only you can do. Delegate everything else.

Let me repeat that: Do only what only you can do. Delegate *everything* else.

That's hard for people. Whether it's due to fear that it won't be done or won't be done right, inhibition about imposing on someone, being controlling, or enjoying manifesting a martyr complex, we hold on to things and will die in a pile doing them.

But even harder than delegation is letting others play on the team. Delegation is letting someone serve you while you play and do your thing, and we all need to do that. But beyond that is bringing others in and letting *them* actually play in the game—and score!

In basketball legend Pat Riley's book on coaching and leadership, he talks about one of the most important and unique players he ever coached—Magic Johnson. One day Riley pulled Magic aside and said, "Why are you the way you are? Why do you give everything away?"

Johnson told him that when he was a little boy, playing youth league basketball in East Lansing, Michigan, his coach took him aside and said, "You're the biggest. You're our best player. You should shoot the ball all the time."

So he did. And he did score most of the points every game. His team won, time after time. But when he looked around at the moment of victory, hoping someone would return that big smile of his, his teammates looked miserable. They felt like nobodies. The coach's game plan was producing wins, but it was bashing the team's feelings of success and significance.

Magic didn't want it to be that way—it was driving a wedge between him and his friends—so he decided to change his style. Instead of scoring all the points, he would draw the defenders and then pass to whoever was open. This helped everyone else get better. He allowed them to experience the same kind of joy and fun that he had in playing the game.

Johnson believed that if he helped everyone around him get what they wanted out of the game, then winning would always follow—and he was right. Riley says that instead of crushing his teammates under his own greatness, Johnson studied their styles and figured out how he, as the man controlling the movement of the ball, could help *them* get the most out of the abilities they had. And Riley says that was when the Lakers' drive to success really began—when Magic was just a kid and learned to let others play in the game.[1]

So pass the ball.

Influences

Sixth, a leader is a person who influences. That means that they motivate, inspire, and encourage.

To motivate means to get people going, to make them want to achieve more and go further. Motivation is having fire and then having everyone else catch fire with you.

To inspire someone is different—it is calling them out to be more than they are. It is helping them want to live differently, to give their lives to something more. For example, you can be motivated by money, but it would be difficult to be inspired by money. John Maxwell or Anthony Robbins may motivate me, but it takes a Mother Teresa to inspire me. Or think of it this way: I can be around someone who motivates me to use my time better, manage my money better, or stay in shape better—all motivational issues—but it takes something else to have me walk away wanting to love more, care more, serve more.

But then a leader throws in the third ingredient: encouragement. I am not sure of its source, but a friend once shared with me the following truism: "A pat on the back, though only a few vertebrae removed from a kick in the pants, is miles ahead in results." One of the biggest truths is that what gets recognized, what gets praised, and what gets encouraged is what gets done. In fact, studies have found that verbal affirmation is more valuable to people than money.

But encouragement runs deeper than just a pat on the back. It has to do with being the person who deals in hope. Nothing is more damaging, more harmful, more devastating than a negative, pessimistic attitude. If a leader has that, they are not a leader. I'm not talking about a refusal of reality—that's denial, and it will kill an organization, with the leader saying "Things are fine" while they go right off the edge. What I mean by hope is that you can look at the cup as being half full or half empty, and it makes a world of difference which one you choose.

I once read of an economist who was asked to talk to a group of businesspeople. At the beginning of her address, she tacked up a big sheet of white paper. Then she made a black spot on the paper with her pencil and asked a man in the front row what he saw.

The man replied promptly, "A black spot."

The speaker asked every person in the room the same question, and each answered, "I see a little black spot."

The speaker said, "Yes, there is a little black spot, but none of you mentioned the big sheet of white paper. And that's my speech."

And that's the speech of a leader: "Here's the white paper—there's more going on than just the black spot." And encouraging people in that way is more important than you can possibly imagine. Sometimes it's not our problems that need changing but our perspectives. It's not our circumstances that are at fault but our outlook. And that's what a leader provides.

Develops Other Leaders

The final thing a leader does is develop other leaders. Effective leaders create a leadership culture that develops those around them. As you build your teams, you should be singling out a small group of people from within that team that you are grooming and equipping for leadership.

The more leaders you develop, the more leaders you unleash.

The more leaders are unleashed, the more the church reaches its full redemptive potential.

But there's more at hand with this than merely leadership development—there is also the issue of leadership replacement. You are not going to be in your role forever, nor should you be. Who will take your place?

I once met with a group of senior leaders from some of the better-known churches in the nation. The senior pastor who led our discussion, whose name would be known to virtually anyone in American Christianity, said that he was targeting for strategic investment a group of young staff who were willing to commit to the church for an extended season. He would do all he could to pour himself into them and facilitate their ministries. If they felt called to be a senior pastor, so be it; he would help them reach that goal when they were ready or even groom them to take over his role. But one thing was nonnegotiable for his eventual, inevitable replacement: that person would come from within the organization.

That's one fortunate set of young leaders. But it is also one wise senior leader.

24

Community, Cause, and Corporation

Epaphroditus, my brother, fellow worker and fellow soldier.

Philippians 2:25

What, exactly, is a church? If you think it's a one-dimensional, simplistic enterprise, then you are in for a rude awakening. Or, more likely, you are experiencing enormous tensions and you don't have a clue as to the source.

The truth is that a church is a complex entity that has at least three dimensions: it is a community, a cause, and corporation.[1] And knowing how to focus on each one, not to mention balance them against each other, is one of the most decisive tasks you will ever engage in.

I'm not making these dimensions up. In Philippians, Paul calls Epaphroditus his brother (community), his worker (corporation), and his fellow soldier (cause). This one man was all three to Paul—and people are often all three to you.

For example, think about the church as community. Paul once counseled Timothy to relate to older men as fathers, younger women as sisters, and older women as mothers (1 Tim. 5:1–2). When talking about the church as a cause, the New Testament tends to use military metaphors; think of the armor detailed in the sixth chapter of Ephesians. The church is also an institution with a corporate dynamic, with officers such as pastors/elders, deacons, and those with the gift of administration.

Why is this so important to grasp? If you are in community with someone, then you are a family. If you are in a cause together, then you are an army. If you are in a corporation together, then you are a business. These three dimensions are vastly different from each other in more than just metaphor— they have different core values, different key persons, different ways of entrance and exit, and varying ways of payback.

Consider values. In a community, the greatest values are, arguably, love, loyalty, and mutual support. In a cause, the greatest value is winning. In a corporation, it is effectiveness. Could there be some tension between love and winning, or love and effectiveness?

Or think about roles. In a community, the roles fall into such things as father, mother, brother; in a cause, it would be general, lieutenant, or sergeant. In a corporation, one thinks of a CEO, a president, or an employee. You relate to someone as father in a vastly different way than you do as either general or CEO. Approaching someone as an employee is not the same as approaching them as a brother.

And think of the tension between these three when it comes to key people or heroes. In a community, the key people are often the ones the community rallies around, meaning the weakest. Think of the way a family revolves around a newborn. In a cause, the heroes are the ones who are the most committed. In a corporation, the most honored are usually the most productive.

And perhaps most tricky of all, think of how you exit each of these dimensions. In terms of leaving a community, well, you don't. You are part of a family, or family of origin, forever. You can't ever really leave. When it comes to a cause, you have to desert or, if honorable, die in the effort. In a corporation, you either quit, are fired, or retire.

Starting to get dizzy with the complexities? Sorry to pile it on, but we haven't even arrived at the tough part.

Think about knowing which hat to wear. Someone is not performing well at all, but you know that part of it is based on personal issues in their life. Do you wear the corporate hat of performance or the community hat of concern? In truth, it might be both. They may need a word from you as their general to pick up their pace for the cause and also need a father figure at a moment of weakness.

Let's move the conversation to the macro level. What about these dimensions for the church as a whole? This is critical. Most leaders have a tendency toward one or more of these dimensions. They are more community oriented or cause oriented. Seldom does one person have all three in good balance. Most who are close to me would tell you that I have a large cause component and a healthy corporate dynamic, but I have to work hard on the community part.

But it's not just people—it's the church as a whole. This is the macro part. If the church is oriented primarily to the cause, then it will leave in its wake a trail of burned-out bodies of those who gave their lives to the effort but had little supporting them along the way. If they are oriented toward the corporate side of things, then they will be efficient and organized—and dead, dry, and formulaic. If they lean toward community too much, then they will turn inward and rarely reach their growth potential. After all, the point is to know everyone, right?

Two big lessons: know and work the three dimensions, and compensate for where you are naturally weak or strong.

First let's talk in terms of knowing and working the three dimensions. At Meck, we've learned to put this into our vocabulary. I'll talk with someone and say, "Listen, I've got my corporate hat on with this, just so you know." That helps them receive it in that light and not be offended that I didn't have my community or cause hat on. It cuts both ways, of course. A staff person may come in to see me to admit a performance breakdown but say, "Listen, can I talk about this with a community hat on for a minute?" A good leader is able to switch between the hats with ease and knows which one to wear for which setting. Sometimes it's tough, like when someone is clearly in need of community but you can no longer let their life issues impact the corporate dynamic. Sometimes the most community-oriented thing you can do is help them transition away from vocational ministry so that they can address their personal issues in a less demanding environment.

And handling the natural tendency of the church? It's simple—compensate. If you are naturally more community oriented, surround yourself with cause-driven staff and volunteers. Or if you are averse to the corporate side of things, find people who aren't.

But regardless, make no mistake, the church is all three: a community, a cause, and a corporation. Your job is to know which hat to wear—and when—and to keep your church from wearing just one.

25

Time Control

Seventy years are given to us!
   Some may even reach eighty. . . .
Teach us to make the most of our time,
   so that we may grow in wisdom.

Psalm 90:10, 12 NLT

Ministry sometimes seems at war with time management. To begin with, the work is never done. You never reach a point where the word "finished" seems pronounceable. When do you finish fixing marriages? Finish reaching the unchurched in your area? Finish up all the Sundays? If you work at Apple, you have project deadlines, product launches, and end-of-year quotas. You know when you're done. Not in ministry. Your job is to make Christ known to the world and repair the damage of sin in people's lives. You lead an organization that is attempting to end poverty, hunger, homelessness, shame, guilt, loneliness, despair, divorce, racism, and low self-esteem.

I'm getting tired just writing it out.

And not only is the task never-ending, but there isn't a clear sense of "clocking out" to catch your breath. No five o'clock whistle, "Thank God it's Friday," or the-boss-be-darned vacation days. Instead, the work and its demands seep into every crevice of the day. Particularly in single staff situations, you can be called upon for any reason and summoned at any time.

This leads to one of two scenarios: laziness or workaholism. Laziness is possible because time really is yours to manage, and you can slip into a reactionary mode where you only do what you have to do. Workaholism can take hold because there is never an end to what can be done. Neither is what you want. So how do you order your time? Here's some of what I have learned.

Know When You Are Going to Write

First, know when you are going to write. Few things are more important to set aside and then protect than the time you will need to prepare messages. For me, it's Tuesdays (all day), Wednesday mornings, and Thursday mornings. A full two days of my week, around fifteen to twenty hours, are spent on this task. Like anyone else, I need less time some weeks, more time other weeks, but I have these times set aside, with the all-day Tuesday effort among the most protected turf on my calendar.

Have an Office, and Have a Study

This may not sound like a time management principle, but it is. I've learned to have a home office where I write and keep my books and an office on the church's campus where

I meet with people, have meetings, and fulfill the leadership responsibilities of my role. This protects my writing time from being invaded by the office and, of course, keeps the leadership time from being assailed by writing responsibilities. I've even divided my library accordingly, with most of my books on leadership at the office but the bulk of my library that I need for writing (Christian living, biography, history, Old and New Testament commentaries, apologetics, and sociology/culture) at home.

Create Two "Ends"

Next, have an end to each and every week. For me, it's Thursday afternoon. That's when the whistle blows and I walk away from the work.

This means a typical workweek for me would be arriving on the campus on a Saturday afternoon for the rehearsal of the weekend service and then beginning the schedule of services, which for our church involves both Saturday night and Sunday. I spend Mondays at the office for leadership and administrative responsibilities, Tuesdays at home for writing, Wednesday mornings at home for writing with the afternoon back at the office, and finally, Thursday mornings at home writing with the afternoon at the office. Friday is my day off. Many choose a Monday to rest after a full Sunday of events. I'm a Friday guy—it fits in nicely with the chosen end of my workweek.

But as important as the end to the workweek is the end to a season. For me, this is usually around Father's Day in June, with the "new year" resuming the first week or so of August. Those six to eight weeks in between provide the time for my annual summer study break, vacation times, travel—anything but staying involved in the routine of teaching and leadership.

Have a Bias for Action

Too much time is wasted with inactivity. Have a bias for action. The temptation is to have a mentality of "Ready . . . aim . . . aim . . . aim . . ." There comes a time to *fire*. I once had a staff person who would sit around all day daydreaming in front of his laptop. He would come up with ideas and cute acrostics, but he never actually *did* anything. Nothing ever materialized.

Want to save some time? Pull the trigger.

Delegate

One of the biggest time wasters is doing things that others can and should do. We talked about this a bit under "What a Leader Does" (chapter 23), but it bears repeating. There is a difference between doing and delegating. When you "do," you are very busy but not particularly effective. Only do what only you can do!

Three Priorities

I have no idea where I first heard this maxim, but I am confident it is not original with me: "If you have more than three priorities, you have no priorities." The point is that if you try to prioritize too many things, you aren't really prioritizing anything. The point of a priority is that you are setting aside a very small number of things for strategic and preferential investment.

Twice each year I set aside my top three priorities for the next "season" of ministry. I am ruthless about the selection, and then I convey each one to those closest to me—not just for accountability but so that they know how to join with me in making critical time-investment decisions.

Refuse the Tyranny of the Urgent

One of the most important time principles in my life was shaped through a little book I read many years ago by Charles Hummel called *The Tyranny of the Urgent*. When he was young and just starting out in the marketplace, an experienced manager took him aside and gave him some important advice. He said, "Your greatest danger is letting the urgent things crowd out the important."

That little maxim hit Hummel hard; in fact, it changed his life so profoundly that he wrote about it. In his book, Hummel speaks of how we live our lives in constant tension between the urgent and the important.[1] And there is a difference between the two.

Important things don't have to be done today or even this week. They don't scream out for attention. They are things like a visit with a friend, careful study of an important book, or prayer and Bible study. But urgent things scream out at us for attention: answer that phone, respond to that email, make this deadline, catch that plane. The urgent screams for attention and as a result gets it.

But life isn't just the urgent—it is also to be filled with the important, and we should make a conscious decision as to what the important things are. And then we must be disciplined about them, because that's what discipline is about— exerting the self-imposed order on your life that's needed in order to do what does not naturally get done.

The important needs to get done.

Make a "Stop Doing" List

I'm a list person. I write down what I need to do and have several different kinds of to-do lists going at any time. But

I have had to learn about a different kind of list—a "stop doing" list. This is far from original to my thinking, of course, but I am surprised at how seldom it is discussed.

Think of reading. Many would like to resolve that in the coming year they will read more. Those who are savvy about themselves know they will need to sharpen that up a bit and be specific: "I would like to read twenty-five books this year." Some will go further and put the twenty-five books into categories, such as five books in history, five in biography, and so on.

But those who will actually *read* twenty-five books this year will tend to be those who accompany their resolution with a change in lifestyle. It isn't enough to simply want to read more; you have to also decide to spend less time on the internet or watch fewer DVDs.

There are only twenty-four hours in a day, seven days in a week, and fifty-two weeks in a year. Time is finite, which means something has to give. It's not about whether you can read more, exercise more, pray more; it's about whether you will decide to invest your time accordingly. You have the time—it's simply a matter of reallocating it toward what you most want to do and be.

It's All about Discipline

A great deal of our lives—the people we want to become, the impact we want to make—is tied not simply to desire but to whether we will exercise disciplined ambition. *Desire* is simply longing or wishing. *Ambition* has to do with such desire becoming focused on an objective and thus resulting in someone driven toward a particular goal. *Discipline* has to do with a management of life that results in self-control, orderliness, and efficiency.

The life of ministry is a rich opportunity to enact a level of discipline that will allow you to read and write, serve and teach, mentor and lead. The phrase *carpe diem* (Latin for "seize the day") is often employed by those who would encourage us to take hold of time and make the most of it. We have the privilege of being able to actually do it.

Afterword

It's a Wonderful Life

experienced every pastor's secret dream—or at least the secret dream of a lot of pastors.

Most of us loved seminary. We loved learning and idolized our professors. What a life they had! Teaching and writing and reflecting on ministry, God, the Bible, and the church, without the headaches of weddings, deacons' meetings, raising money, or dealing with how regularly Sundays always seem to come.

Our secret fantasy? To be offered a job at a seminary. To teach and to escape. And if we let our fantasy get really out of this world, it would be to be named the president of one.

It happened to me. And like many of you might have, I said yes.

Then I resigned in less than two years and came back to the church I had left. And I am so glad.

In the classic Christmas movie *It's a Wonderful Life*, George Bailey got a chance to see what life would be like if he had never lived. In like manner, I was given a chance to see what life would be like without serving as the pastor of a church. George Bailey learned he wanted to live again. So did I.

As I hope I made clear at the beginning, this is not meant to be disparaging to those who are called to serve in seminaries as professors or administrators. But for those of us who are called to ministry in the local church, please hear me say: *no other vocational pursuit will satisfy.*

If you are really called, then nothing else you will ever try to do will satiate your drive.

I know it's tough. I know there are days you want to quit. Don't. If you do, you'll wish you could go back. I've never yet met anyone who at one time was truly called to the church but did get out of the game who remained glad they left.

You will miss getting a terrific idea for a talk or a series and having the ability to develop it and teach it.

You will miss coming upon a nugget of scriptural insight, tethered to language and historical insights, and being able to share it.

You will miss living in full community with others—young and old, married and single, believer and seeker, black and white.

You will miss being a leader, chasing dreams and building a kingdom vision that reflects the comprehensive vision of the church, and being free to pursue that vision with all vigor and energy without barrier.

You will miss being on the front lines of impacting lives—not just talking about life change but seeing it, experiencing it, making it happen as you cooperate with the Holy Spirit in people's lives.

Simply put, if you are a practitioner and not a theoretician, you will miss the practice.

I caught something on TV one summer that riveted me. It was a one-hour program on the Ironman World Championship triathlon held in Hawaii. It is the premier triathlon competition in the world. And it deserves its name. It involves a swim in the open ocean of over two miles, followed by over one hundred miles of biking, ending with a full marathon run.

What grabbed me about this program wasn't the competition itself but the stories of the people involved, their strength of will, and their fight to the finish. One of the individuals profiled was a woman named Lyn Brooks. She was competing in her *nineteenth* Ironman. She talked about how one year, during the marathon leg of the competition, she left the race and entered an aid tent by the side of the road. Her body was aching, her emotions were drained, and the desire to stop—to just end it all there—was overpowering.

When she entered the tent, she looked over, and sitting on a bench was a man who had also been competing. He was just resting and relaxing, drinking an ice cold beer. Reading her thoughts, he said, "All you have to do is drop out of the race like me."

Suddenly, she said, she realized who he was—he was the devil. She immediately left the tent and reentered the race. Reflecting on the moment filled her eyes with tears. She said, "It was the hardest, and most *glorious*, day of my life."[1]

Stay in the race.

Notes

Introduction

1. Susanne M. Schafer, Associated Press, "Forget Bayonets; Army Busts Abs in Basic Overhaul," *Charlotte Observer*, Wednesday, March 17, 2010.

Chapter 2 The Five C's

1. Jim Collins, *Good to Great* (New York: HarperCollins, 2001), 41–64.

Chapter 3 The Next Next Thing

1. Adam Bryant, "iSee into the Future, Therefore iAm," *New York Times*, July 1, 2007.
2. "Religion among the Millennials," Pew Forum on Religion and Public Life, February 2010, http://pewforum.org/docs/?DocID=510.
3. Stephen Prothero, "Millennials Do Faith and Politics Their Way," *USA Today*, March 29, 2010.
4. Bryant, "iSee into the Future, Therefore iAm."
5. Jim Collins, *How the Mighty Fall* (New York: HarperCollins, 2009), 1.

Chapter 5 It's the Weekend, Stupid

1. 1985 Technical Assistance Research Program (TARP) study for the White House Office of Consumer Affairs.
2. 1988 Technical Assistance Research Program (TARP) study for the White House Office of Consumer Affairs. The actual results regarding why customers did not return to a particular establishment were as follows: 1 percent died, 3 percent moved, 5 percent due to friendship, 9 percent due to competition, 14 percent as a result of product dissatisfaction, and 68 percent as a result of an indifferent, unfriendly employee attitude.

3. *Sister Act*, directed by Emile Ardolino (Burbank, CA: Touchstone Pictures, 1992).

4. Doug Murren, *The Baby Boomerang: Catching Baby Boomers as They Return to Church* (Ventura, CA: Regal, 1990), 188.

5. Rick Warren, *The Purpose-Driven Church* (Grand Rapids: Zondervan, 1995), 283.

6. Harry Lucenay, "Blending the Traditional and the Contemporary," in Joe R. Stacker and Wesley Forbis, eds., *Authentic Worship: Exalting God and Reaching People* (Nashville: Convention Press, 1990), 22.

7. Warren, *Purpose-Driven Church*, 283.

8. Tom Peters and Nancy Austin, *A Passion for Excellence: The Leadership Difference* (New York: Random House, 1985), 99.

9. James Belasco, *Teaching the Elephant to Dance: Empowering Change in Your Organization* (New York: Crown Publishers, 1990), 14.

Chapter 6 Sexual Fences

1. William Martin, *A Prophet with Honor: The Billy Graham Story* (New York: William Morrow, 1991), 107.

2. C. S. Lewis, *Mere Christianity* (New York: Macmillan, 1952), 75.

3. A recent popular book on this idea is Suzy Welch, *10-10-10: A Life-Transforming Idea* (New York: Scribner, 2009).

Chapter 7 Rabies of the Heart

1. Will D. Campbell, *Brother to a Dragonfly* (New York: Continuum, 1987), 181.

2. Gordon MacDonald, *Restoring Your Spiritual Passion* (Guilford, England: Highland Books, 2004), 98.

3. Cornelius Plantinga Jr., *Not the Way It's Supposed to Be* (Grand Rapids: Eerdmans, 1995), 167.

Chapter 9 Forever Young

1. Edward Gibbon, *Decline and Fall of the Roman Empire*, XXXVIII.

2. "Southern Baptists Face Further Decline without Renewed Evangelism Emphasis," *Florida Baptist Witness*, July 28, 2009, http://www.floridabaptistwitness.com/10578.article.

Chapter 10 Hills to Die On

1. Our values are not original to us, meaning these ten, and even some of the phrasing, can be found in other churches that came into existence long before our own.

Chapter 11 Vision Leaks

1. Michael E. Gerber, *The E-Myth Revisited: Why Most Small Businesses Don't Work and What to Do about It* (New York: HarperCollins, 2001), 69.

Chapter 13 Spiritually Hazardous

1. Mother Teresa, *Come Be My Light: The Private Writings of the "Saint of Calcutta,"* ed. and commentary Brian Kolodiejchuck (New York: Doubleday, 2007), 2.

2. Seth Godin, *Seth's Blog*, "Watch the Money," November 30, 2009, http://sethgodin.typepad.com/seths_blog/2009/11/watch-the-money.html.

Chapter 14 It's Not Rocket Science

1. Albert Einstein, quoted in "Autobiographical Notes," *Great Treasury of Western Thought*, ed. Mortimer J. Adler and Charles Van Doren (New York: Bowker, 1977), 1128.

Chapter 15 10-10-80

1. Fred R. Shapiro, ed., *Yale Book of Quotations* (New Haven, CT: Yale University Press, 2006), 618.

Chapter 16 We Are They

1. Shapiro, *Yale Book of Quotations*, 845.

2. On the many stories and commentaries surrounding the slaying of Kitty Genovese, see Michael Dorman's "The Killing of Kitty Genovese" in *Long Island: Our Story* (Melville, New York: Newsday Books, 1998).

3. Associated Press, "Woman Dies after Cries for Help Ignored," *Charlotte Observer*, May 27, 1999.

4. See Malcolm Gladwell, *The Tipping Point* (Boston: Little, Brown and Company, 2000), 27.

5. Ibid., 27.

6. Ibid., 27–28.

7. Ibid.

Chapter 17 Bone Structure

1. *New York Times*, April 4, 1960, quoted in Shapiro, *Yale Book of Quotations*, 668.

2. Philip Howard, *The Death of Common Sense* (New York: Random House, 1994), 11.

3. See Allan Cox with Julie Liesse, *Redefining Corporate Soul* (Chicago: Irwin, 1996), 69.

Chapter 18 Community under Construction

1. Bertrand Russell, *The Analysis of Mind*, "Lecture X," in *Great Treasury of Western Thought*, 493.

2. John Ortberg, *Everybody's Normal Till You Get to Know Them* (Grand Rapids: Zondervan, 2003), 137.

3. Stephen R. Covey, *7 Habits of Highly Effective People* (New York: Simon and Schuster, 1989), 30–31.

4. Tertullian, *The Apology*, AD 197.

Chapter 19 Spiritual Narcissism

1. Christopher Lasch, *The Culture of Narcissism* (London: W. W. Norton, 1978), 5.

Chapter 21 Safe People

1. Henry Cloud and John Townsend, *Safe People* (Grand Rapids: Zondervan, 1996), 28–39.

Chapter 22 PKs

1. See Tim Hansel, *What Kids Need Most in a Dad* (Grand Rapids: Revell, 2002), 75.

Chapter 23 What a Leader Does

1. Pat Riley, *The Winner Within* (New York: Berkeley Books, 1994), 36–37.

Chaper 24 Community, Cause, and Corporation

1. The idea of the church as community, cause, and corporation was relayed to me many years ago by Jim Dethmer, who used to be a pastor and now works as a leadership consultant to both nonprofits and marketplace endeavors and who has given me permission to share his premise with others. This idea initially appeared in his article "Moving in the Right Circles," *Leadership Journal* 13, no. 4 (Fall 1992): 86–91.

Chapter 25 Time Control

1. Charles E. Hummel, *Tyranny of the Urgent*, rev. ed. (Downers Grove, IL: InterVarsity Press, 1999).

Afterword

1. Adapted from NBC TV coverage of the 1998 Ironman World Championship in Hawaii, rebroadcast on Sunday, July 25, 1999.

James Emery White (PhD) is the founding and senior pastor of Mecklenburg Community Church in Charlotte, North Carolina, and president of Serious Times, a ministry which explores the intersection of faith and culture and hosts the website churchandculture.org, where he blogs regularly. Dr. White is also ranked adjunctive professor of theology and culture on the Charlotte campus of Gordon-Conwell Theological Seminary, which he also served as their fourth president, and author of over a dozen books which have been translated into ten languages. His commitment to local church ministry includes service as Distinguished Professor of Pastoral Ministry at Anderson University and consulting editor to *Leadership Journal*.

Rethinking
the
Church

by James Emery White

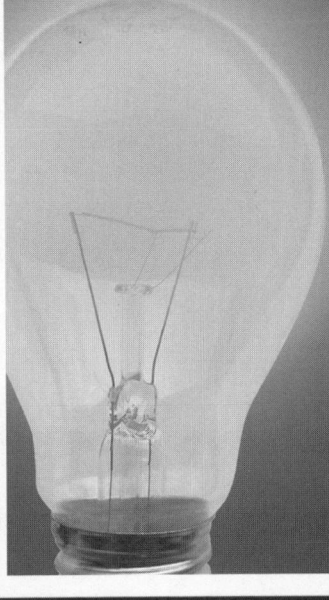

"I wish this book had been around when I was an atheist and started to seek God. It's a no-nonsense, practical, insightful guide that will help all seekers in their quest for spiritual truth. If you're investigating whether there's any substance to the Christian faith, you must read this important book."

—Lee Strobel, author, *The Case for Christ*

"If you've been looking for one book to put in the hands of someone exploring faith, this is it."

—Bill Hybels, senior pastor,
Willow Creek Community Church

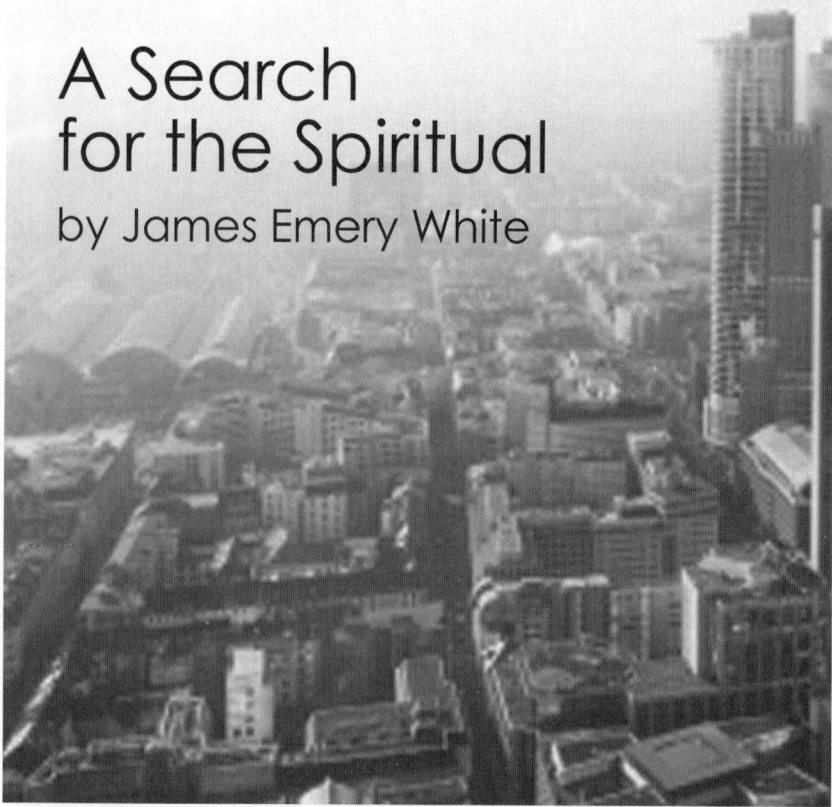

A Search
for the Spiritual
by James Emery White